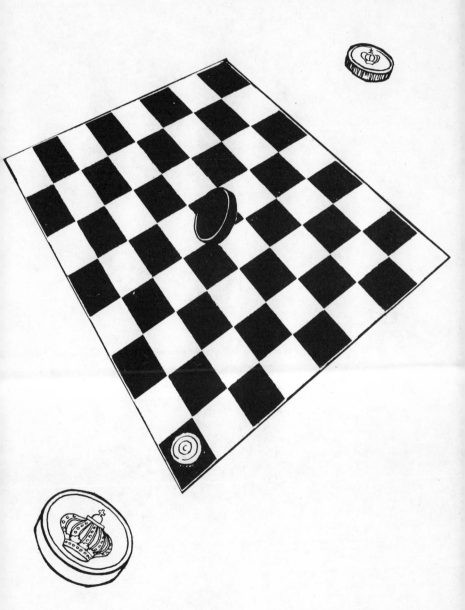

How to Win at Checkers

By FRED REINFELD

Everyone thinks he can play checkers—and usually does. But it is an often overlooked fact that checkers, when *properly* played, can offer as much of a challenge as a chess game. Top-Notch Checkers is almost an entirely different game from the checkers every youngster knows.

This book is for players who have yet to realize the artistic beauty of the game. Because of a new style of diagram with numbered squares, every step is made absolutely clear without groping so the beginner learns more, learns faster and enjoys it.

Fred Reinfeld, master chess player, for the first time turns his vast knowledge of board strategy to the game of checkers, and explains how you can increase your playing strength enormously. He develops fine points and winning methods previously unknown to the amateur, and in the process he whets your enthusiasm for the game.

Included in the contents are basic rules and variations of the game; traps, shots and star moves; basic endgames, opening attacks and safest defenses; and the theory of the opposition, which enables you to tell at a glance who has "the move"—the key to victory or defeat.

TOP-NOTCH CHECKERS shows the same sympathetic understanding which Mr. Reinfeld brings to his innumerable chess books, which have won international acclaim.

Howard Sur

Fred Reinfeld is an author extraordinary. Some of his many readers call him a "genius," and all recognize his versatility and talent. He is probably the most prolific American writer living today, author of about 75 books (more than he can count, he says).

Mr. Reinfeld is a native New Yorker. He began his career in chess while still in his teens, became intercollegiate champion, New York State champion, and winner of the Manhattan Club and Marshall Club championship matches, beating such worthy opponents as Sammy Reshevsky and Reuben Fine. He went on to become one of the world's great chess masters.

Since retiring from active play, he has continued to write brilliant analyses of chess for players on all levels.

When Mr. Reinfeld's biography of "The Great Chess Masters" was published, the *New York Times* said: "Mr. Reinfeld is a sympathetic analyst of sheer human quality. He is a man of letters who deserves an accolade for his masterly performance."

He has also turned out equally fine books on coin collecting, geology, and science.

How to Win at Checkers

How to Win at Checkers

1967 EDITION

By FRED REINFELD

Wilshire Book Company
8721 Sunset Blvd.
Hollywood, California, 90069

OTHER BOOKS BY FRED REINFELD

CONTENTS

1. Checker Fundamentals

To play checkers badly is quite easy; and that is the way most people *do* play it.

Even if you don't play a perfect game of checkers, you can still enjoy the game. But checkers as the experts play it, with all its richness of ideas and exquisite economy of force, is much more fun. It is always more gratifying to play expertly and to win, than it is to flounder. That is why this book has been written. Its purpose is to enable you to play like an expert so that you will derive greater enjoyment and keener appreciation of the beauty of the game.

Checkers is played by two opponents. The checkers are placed on a board which has 64 squares, colored alternately light and dark. Only the *dark* squares are used.

Each player starts with 12 men. One set of men is known as *Black,* the other as *White.* (In practice, the two most common color combinations are black for the dark color and red for the light—or, sometimes, red for the dark and white for the light color.)

Whatever the actual colors used, Black is the official name for the dark color and White for the light color.

Note that when you set up the men at the beginning of a game, a dark single-corner square is at each player's left.

In order to describe and record moves, it is customary to

number the 32 squares on the checkerboard which are in use during a game. Diagram 1 shows how these squares are numbered.

Diagram 1 (*the numbered board*)

BLACK

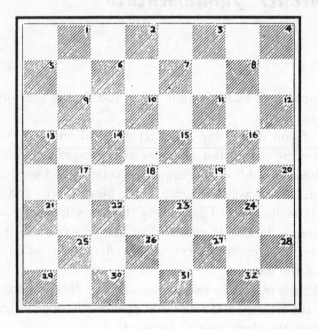

WHITE

To record a move, you give the number of the square on which a man stands, followed by a dash and the number of the square to which it moves. For example, 11—15 means, "the man on 11 moves to 15."

In this connection, here is a word of advice which will help you become a proficient student of checkers and will also increase your playing skill enormously while at the same time giving you a finer imaginative grasp of the game. When you buy a checkerboard, get one with *numbered squares*. These are available in many stores and cost no more than the ordinary, unnumbered boards.

Constant use of the numbered checkerboard will make the numbering system second nature to you, so that you will be able to read off the moves effortlessly and concentrate fully on the material you are studying.

If you find it impossible to obtain a numbered checkerboard, you can number the squares on an ordinary checkerboard to achieve the same effect.

Here are some points about the checker notation that you will find useful. The actual moves played are arranged in two vertical columns, with Black's moves in the left column and White's moves in the right column.

When you are studying the play following a diagramed position, it is a good idea to first go through the main play in the columns (described as the text play or the text continuation). This will give you a good over-all picture of the sequence of moves and their main objective. Then, when you have studied this part, you can turn to the notes to the play and consider the alternative moves that have been discussed in the course of the play.

When these alternative lines are given, the sequence of moves is in sentence or paragraph form. In such cases, in order to make it easier for the inexperienced reader to follow the play, all Black moves are preceded by three dots.

You will also need to be familiar with the following symbols:

!	Good move
!!	Very fine move
?	Weak move
??	Very weak move
(K)	Becomes a King

Diagram 2 shows how the checkerboard looks when the men are set up ready for starting play.

Diagram 2 (*the opening position*)

BLACK

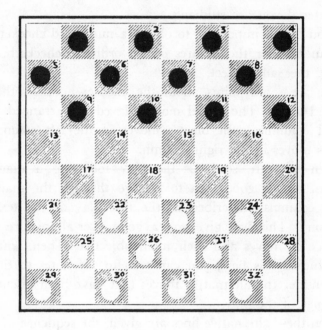

WHITE

Note that the Black men are set out on squares 1 to 12. The White men occupy squares 21 to 32.

All these men move in a *diagonally forward* direction. Black men move toward the White side ("down the page"), while White men move toward the Black side ("up the page").

Each man can move forward one square to the right or left (to another dark square), provided that the square is unoccupied.

Black always makes the first move. Which moves are available to him at the very start? Obviously, at the very beginning, only four of his men can move. These are the men on 9, 10, 11, and 12. The moves available to Black, then, are . . . 9—13 or . . . 9—14; or . . . 10—14 or . . . 10—15; or . . . 11—15 or 11—16; or . . . 12—16.

Once Black has made his first move, White makes *his* first move. And so the game goes on, each man moving in turn. To make his first move, White has a choice of moving any of the men on 21, 22, 23, or 24.

You win a game of checkers by capturing all your opponent's men or putting them in a position where they are all blocked and cannot make any move.

Diagram 3 (*Black to play*)

BLACK

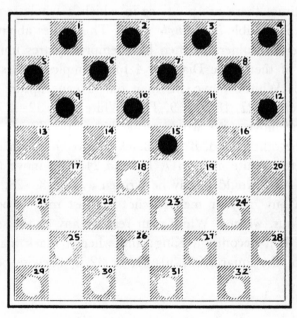

WHITE

A basic rule of the game is: In checkers, CAPTURES ARE COMPULSORY. Of course, if more than one capture is possible, you have the option of making the capture which you deem most advantageous.

Now, let us see how capturing is achieved. Diagram 3 illustrates this point. Black has played . . . 11—15 and White has played 22—18 in reply. (This is known as the "Single Corner" Opening.)

It is Black's turn to play. His man on 15 captures the White man on 18 by leaping over it and coming to rest on 22. The captured man on 18 is removed from the board.

White now captures the Black man on 22. White can do this by either 25—18 or 26—17. Each side has captured a man and thus material is even.

Clearly, in order for a capture to be possible, the square immediately behind the man to be captured must be empty.

Sometimes there are positions in which a whole sequence of captures is possible *in a single move*. This comes about because a number of vulnerable men have empty squares immediately in back of them. See Diagram 4 for examples of this.

If it is White's move, his man on 32 can capture all three Black men on 27, 18, and 9. Thus White plays 32—23—14—5 all in one move. (We would write this simply 32—5.)

On the other hand, if it is Black's move, his man on 3 can capture the White men on 7, 15, and 24. This move (. . . 3—10—19—28) would simply be written as . . . 3—28.

When any of your men reaches the last row, it becomes a King. Thus, when a White man reaches any of the squares 1, 2, 3, or 4, it becomes a King; and when a Black man arrives at any of the squares 29, 30, 31, or 32, it likewise becomes a King.

Diagram 4

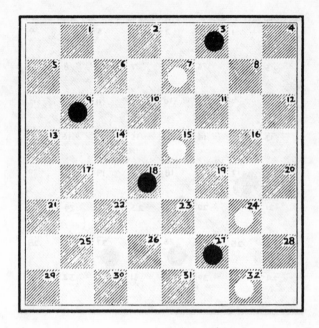

To show that you have a King, another man of the same color is placed on top of the newly "crowned" man.

Kings are extremely powerful because (although they can move only one square at a time) they can move *forward or backward*. They can also capture forward or backward, and can make multiple captures in a single move if the opponent's men are set out in a vulnerable formation. In making such multiple captures they can move backward *and* forward all in one move. This is shown in Diagram 5.

Diagram 5

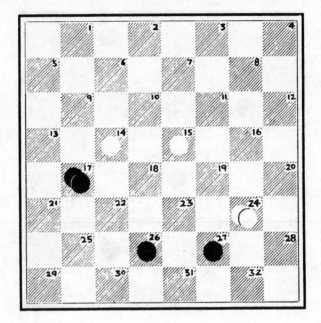

WHITE

If it is Black's move, his King on 17 can capture the White men on 14 and 15 and the White King on 24 *all in one move.* Black plays . . . 17—10—19—28 (written . . . 17—28) in a single move. This wins at once, as it removes all the remaining White men.

On the other hand, if it is White's turn to play, his King on 24 can capture the Black men on 27 and 26 and the Black King on 17. This move would be 24—31—22—13 (written 24—13), and it would win the game at once as all the Black men would disappear from the board.

Capturing in checkers, as you will see, is a *duty* as well as a *privilege.* The beginner easily forgets that there are times when capturing is most unwelcome. Thus, you may have to capture a hostile man only to find that in consequence you lose two—or maybe even three—of your own men in reply.

This suggests two thoughts. One is that when it is your turn to move, you must use some foresight to watch out for traps. Can your opponent answer your intended move with a trap that will offer you a man and enable him to get two in return? (This is the famous "two-for-one shot," described in detail in the next chapter.)

Your second thought on this subject should be that in situations where it is your turn to play, you may be in position to execute the two-for-one shot yourself. That is, you may have an opportunity to offer one of your own men, forcing your opponent to capture, and then proceed to capture two of his men in reply.

Many games, especially those between beginners, are decided in this way.

Diagram 6 (*what result?*)

BLACK

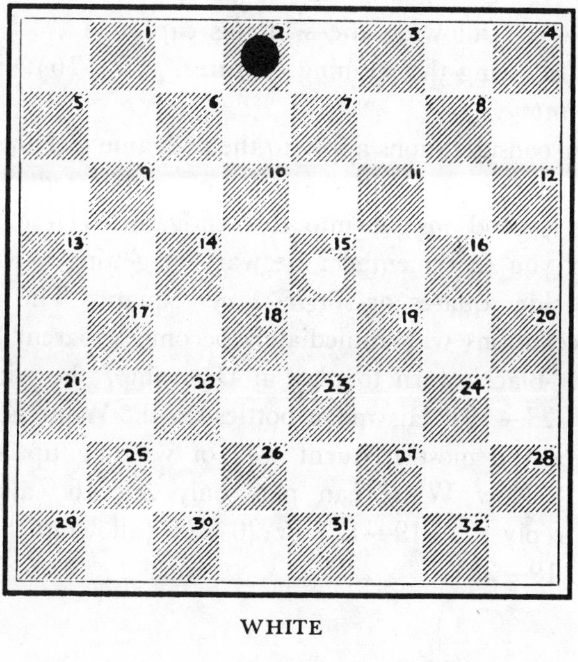

WHITE

Occasionally games end in a *draw;* no decisive result is achieved. (The percentage of draws among well-matched experts is much higher than it is among inexperienced players who are likely to "blow" the game with one catastrophically bad move.) The draw generally becomes apparent toward the end of the game when material is even and greatly simplified and neither side can force a win.

It would be a great mistake, however, for the beginner to assume that *all* greatly simplified positions where material is even are necessarily drawn. Consider the situation in Diagram 6, for example.

If it is White's turn to play, he moves 15—10! and wins on the spot, as Black must play . . . 2—6 (allowing the winning capture 10—1), or . . . 2—7 (allowing the winning capture 10—3). We say that White has *the move*—he controls Black's last move. (See the discussion beginning on page 46.)

On the other hand, if it is Black's turn to move in Diagram 6, he plays . . . 2—7! and wins at once. For White must either play 15—10 (allowing the winning capture . . . 7—14), or 15—11 (allowing the winning capture . . . 7—16). Here Black has *the move*.

Similar considerations apply to the endgame of King vs. King, except that the possibilities are more complicated. Diagram 7 gives us a good insight into this endgame. (Here is a basic point for you to remember: be wary of getting a King boxed into the side squares or *single-corner* squares. The reason for these precautions will immediately become apparent.)

If it is Black's turn to play in Diagram 7, he wins at once with . . . 23—19! His move bottles up the White King. (This is perhaps the most frequent way of winding up a game of checkers.) Now White can play only 20—16 (allowing the winning reply . . . 19—12) or 20—24 (allowing the winning reply . . . 19—28).

Diagram 7 (*what result?*)

BLACK

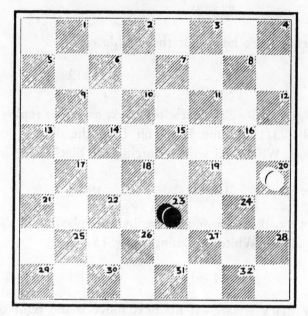

WHITE

Now, suppose that in Diagram 7 it is *White's* move. What should the result be? White will win *or* draw, depending on whether Black makes the right or wrong reply. If Black makes the right reply, he draws. If he makes the wrong reply, he loses.

Both procedures lead to endgames of fundamental importance.

First, let us see what happens if Black plays correctly.

BLACK	WHITE
....	20—24

Now Black's proper course is to head for the *double corner* made up of 1 and 5. Once he gets access to this corner, he is safe. (On the other hand, after . . . 23—26?? White wins by 24—19 or 24—27 as Black never reaches the double corner.)

23—18!   ....

Correct. Black heads for the double corner.

....   24—19

Now . . . 18—22?? loses for Black, as White replies 19—15! (or 19—23!) heading Black off from the double corner. (In that case, White will win by forcing the Black King into a side square.)

18—14!   19—15

Here too Black can go wrong by now playing . . . 14—17??, which allows White's winning reply 15—18!

14—9!   ....

Now Black is safe—if his next move is the right one.

....   15—10

The last chance for Black to go wrong: if he now plays . . . 9—13??, White wins with 10—14, bottling up the Black King, which will be captured next move.

9—5!   ....

This establishes the draw, as Black can play . . . 5—1 followed by . . . 1—5 followed by endless repetition of these moves.

Now let us return to the position of Diagram 7, and see how Black *loses by force* if he answers 20—24 incorrectly.

BLACK	WHITE
....	20—24
23—26??	....

This is wrong. White must now win.

....	24—19

Here 24—27 also wins for White. (Play out all the alternative lines to make sure you understand the winning process in all its detail.)

26—22	....

If instead . . . 26—31, White wins at once with 19—23.

....	19—23

If Black now tries 22—25, 23—26 (23—18 also wins); . . . 25—29 (. . . 25—21 loses to the same reply), 26—22 and Black is trapped in the single corner.

22—17	23—18!

Just to make sure you understand the winning process, note that 23—26? would be all wrong, as Black could then run away to the double corner with . . . 17—14! or . . . 17—13!

17—13	....

Or . . 17—21, 18—22 and White wins.

....	18—14

White wins. Study this ending until you have mastered it thoroughly, for it is one of the basic winning procedures in checkers.

You are now familiar with the rules of checkers and with some of the elementary winning methods. We are ready to study some of the simple checker tactics which are at the heart of winning checker play.

2. Winning Checker Tactics

It is not easy for the beginner to realize that the *compulsory* nature of checker captures profoundly affects the tactics used in the game.

The point is this: since you know your opponent must accept any capturing opportunities you set before him, you can plan certain sequences that will win material for you or have other favorable consequences.

Suppose, for example, you could offer one of your men in such a way that when your opponent captures it, you will have a position in which you can win *two* men in return.

This is, in fact, the most common tactical stroke in checkers—the two-for-one shot. Diagram 8 shows how it is done.

The possibility of a two-for-one shot is suggested here by Black's vulnerable diagonal formation.

BLACK	WHITE
....	20—16!
11—20	18—4(K)

The two-for-one shot. White wins easily.

Even a three-for-one shot is possible—more spectacular, but less likely. Again, the diagonal set-up gives the show away. (See Diagram 9.)

Diagram 8 (*White to play and win*)

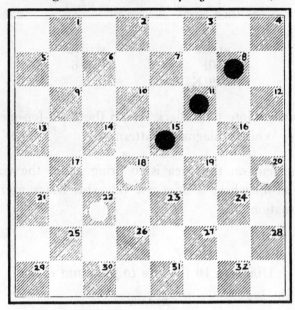

Diagram 9 (*Black to play and win*)

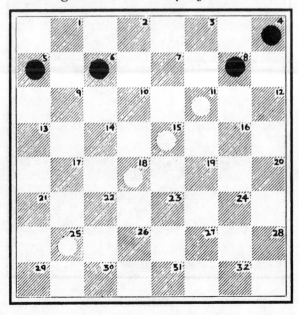

Here Black "pitches" the man on 6 to win. (A pitch in checkers is a sacrifice.)

BLACK	WHITE
6—10!	15—6
8—29(K)	....

Black wins. Note how Black set up the three-for-one shot by weakening White's diagonal pattern.

A refinement on this idea is to bring about the vulnerable diagonal set-up where it does not yet exist. Diagram 10 shows such a situation.

Diagram 10 (*White to play and win*)

BLACK

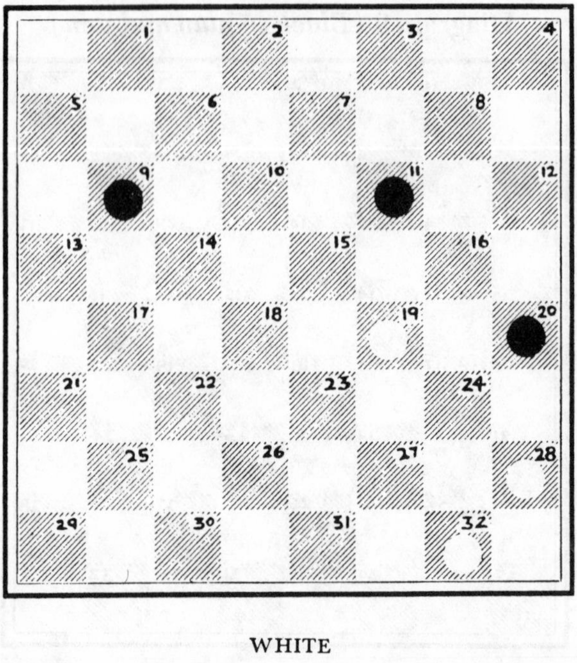

WHITE

White has a three-for-two shot by playing the correct first move. Black's moves are all forced replies.

BLACK	WHITE
....	19—15!

And not 28—24? *first,* for after . . . 20—27 in reply, White must recapture 32—23, spoiling the intended shot. In fact, Black then continues . . . 9—14 winning.

11—18	28—24
20—27	32—5

White wins. Now we can appreciate the power and ingenuity of his opening sacrifice 19—15!

Diagram 11 (*White to play and win*)

BLACK

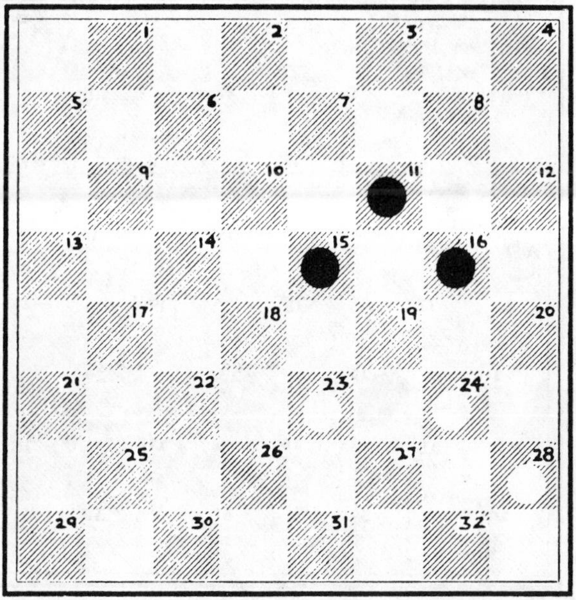

WHITE

Another form of the two-for-one shot is shown in Diagram 11.

Again White begins by forcing a capture.

BLACK	WHITE
....	24—19!
15—24	28—12

White wins. His two-for-one shot was made possible by Black's forced capture.

In Diagram 12 we see the same idea operating in a much more refined form.

Diagram 12 (*White to play and win*)

BLACK

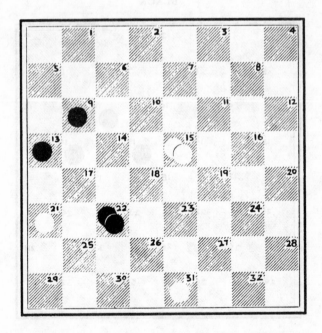

WHITE

White's first move confronts Black with a hidden menace.

BLACK	WHITE
....	21—17!

If Black sees the threat, he can play . . . 9—14, but in that case White wins easily after 17—10.

22—25	17—14!
9—18	15—29

White wins. This is an impressive example of how the obligation to capture can prove disastrous.

Diagram 13 (*Black to play and win*)

BLACK

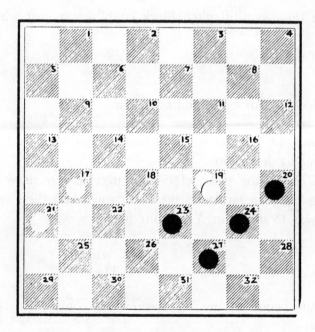

WHITE

The two-for-one shot often turns up as a winning resource in what would otherwise prove to be a troublesome position. Diagram 13 provides a spectacular example.

Black must lose the man on 23 or the man on 24. As the beginner sees it, there is nothing to be done, and he must reconcile himself to the loss. The more experienced player tries to figure out how he can turn the coming capture to his advantage.

BLACK	WHITE
27—31 (K) !	....

Obviously White cannot choose 19—26 now, as . . . 31—13 in reply wins at once. So he selects the other capture.

	19—28
...,....	
20—24!!	....

With this beautiful pitch Black establishes a neat win.

	28—26
....	
31—13	....

Black wins. An exquisite line of play.

In Diagram 14 also we see a fantastic pitch which leads the opponent to destruction.

Black is on the point of establishing an easy draw by advancing his man on 18 to the King row. And there seems to be no way to stop him. Yet White finds a way.

BLACK	WHITE
....	11—15!!

To the beginner, this bit of fireworks comes as a complete surprise.

19—10	28—24!

Diagram 14 (*White to play and win*)

BLACK

WHITE

Everything falls into place for a killing three-for-two shot.

20—27	32—7

White wins. A delightful bit of sly tactics, in which White's first startling move shows what imagination can achieve in checkers.

In Diagram 15 White's winning play has an even more mysterious prelude.

White is so far behind in material, that he seems to be hopelessly lost. Actually, he can force a scintillating win.

Diagram 15 (*White to play and win*)

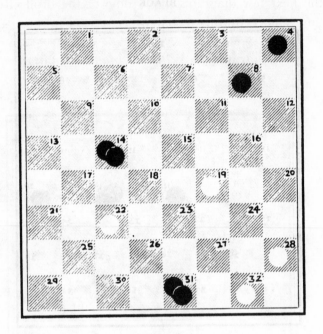

WHITE

BLACK	WHITE
....	22—18!!

Sacrificing two men, to begin with.

| 14—16 | 32—27! |

Setting up a delightful multiple shot.

| 31—24 | 28—3(K) |

White wins. Remarkable play, which shows the amazing opportunities that lurk in harmless-looking positions.

34 • Winning Checker Tactics •

Some of the most spectacular tactical effects occur when you block your opponent's men in the corner squares. Diagram 16 and the next few diagrams show some of the droll effects that you can achieve by this technique.

Diagram 16 (*White to play and win*)

BLACK

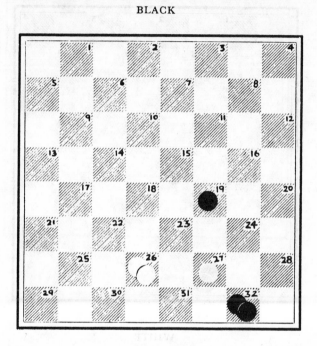

WHITE

White's first move is incomprehensible to those unfamiliar with corner blocking tactics.

BLACK	WHITE
....	27—24!
19—28	26—23!

The point. Black has nothing left but . . . 32—27, whereupon White wins with 23—32, leaving Black without a move.

In Diagram 17 we see a much more refined version of the same idea.

Diagram 17 (*White to play and win*)

BLACK

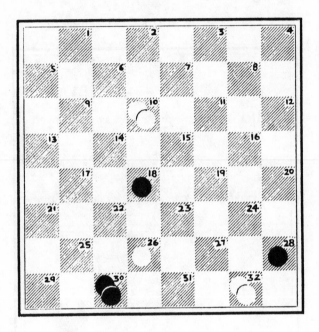

WHITE

This is a highly instructive position because it cannot be solved by "good common sense." The plausible-looking moves get White nowhere.

White's man on 26 is attacked. What is he to do about it?

If he plays the banal 26—23; . . . 18—27, 32—23; Black simply continues . . . 28—32(K) and the game is a clear draw.

And on 10—15; . . . 30—23, 15—22; . . . 23—19, 22—18; . . . 19—24, 18—15; . . . 24—20, 15—19 Black slips out with . . . 20—24.

Instead, relying on the double corner block, White plays an amazing move:

BLACK	WHITE
....	10–14!!

This looks nonsensical, as Black captures on 23 and covers the attacked man on 18.

30–23	....

But now a second sacrifice:

....	32–27!
23–32	14–23

White wins, thanks to the double corner predicament of Black's forces; this is the identical concluding position of the previous example.

Diagram 18 (*White to play and win*)

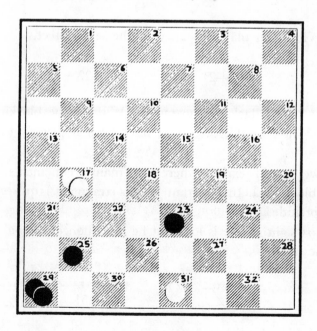

WHITE

Strictly speaking, the term "block" applies to positions where the trapped pieces cannot move altogether. This will be illustrated in Diagram 19, but in Diagram 18 we have an example in which Black loses (despite his numerical superiority) because of the unfortunate immobility of his forces.

In order to bring about the position he wants, White must pitch the man on 31.

BLACK	WHITE
....	31—26!
23—30(K)	17—21
30—26	....

Catastrophic—but forced!

	21—23
....	23—18
29—25	

Or White can play 23—26 with the same effect.

25—21	18—22

White wins. Black has no moves! Without the blocking possibility, White would, of course, have been hopelessly lost.

As we would expect, there are many refinements of the corner block idea. In Diagram 19 this stratagem requires a very clever prelude.

At first sight White is lost, but he hits upon an heroic way to turn the tables.

BLACK	WHITE
....	19—15!

Sacrificing two men to set up the single corner block.

Diagram 19 (*White to play and win*)

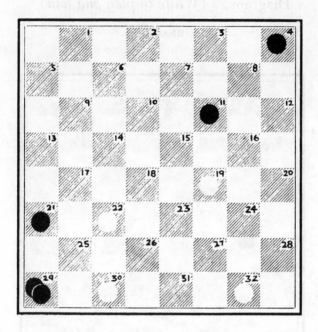

11—25	32—27

Now White wins because he has *the move*.

4—8	27—23
8—11	23—19

White wins. Black must let his last mobile man be captured, and is then left without moves. This is an impressive example of the single corner block.

Here is a refinement on a two-for-one shot, in somewhat unconventional form.

Diagram 20 (*White to play and win*)

BLACK

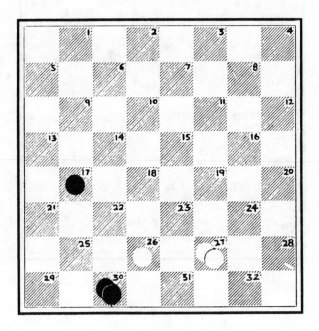

WHITE

Naturally White disdains the colorless 26—23, which leads to a lifeless draw. Instead:

BLACK	WHITE
....	26—22!
17—26	27—31!

White wins. Black must play . . . 30—25, allowing White to reply with the devastating 31—29.

The beginner often overlooks the fact that in even endings with Kings, it is possible to win as shown in Diagram 7. Take Diagram 21 as a simple but impressive example of an even position that can be reduced to a forced win.

Diagram 21 (*White to play and win*)

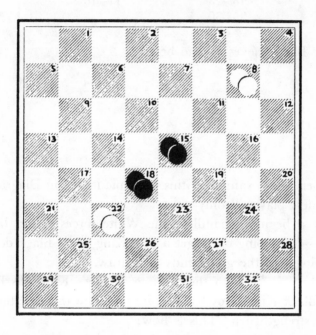

WHITE

Making proper use of this economical possibility often means the difference between victory and defeat, or, as in this case, between a clever victory and a careless draw.

The inexperienced player, seeing that his King at 22 is threatened, might simply move it away and conclude, "It's a hopeless draw!" Actually, White has an easy win!

BLACK	WHITE
....	8—11!

Giving Black a choice of two captures, either one of which loses quickly. Thus, if . . . 15—8, 22—15; . . . 8—12 (any other Black move is answered conclusively in the same way), 15—11 and wins.

BLACK	WHITE
18—25	11—18
25—30	....

Other Black moves are no better.

BLACK	WHITE
....	18—22

White wins.

An even finer example of this principle is seen in Diagram 22. Thoughtless play will only draw.

Many a beginner handling the White forces would happily play 15—11?, going on to get a new King while Black does the same thing and the game ends in a draw.

But there is more to the position. White's King has bottled up the Black King. How can White maintain this situation and actually strengthen it? This is how:

BLACK	WHITE
....	10—14!

By attacking the man on 17, White gives Black no time to free his King.

BLACK	WHITE
17—22	15—10!

Splendid! Note the economy of force applied by White: the man on 10 imprisons a *King*.

Diagram 22 (*White to play and win*)

BLACK

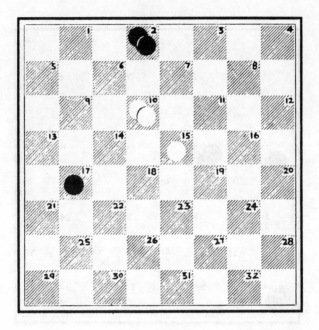

WHITE

And now for the second point: Black will get another King, to be sure, but White will be able to trap this King.

22—26	14—18
26—31(K)	18—23

White wins. Both Black Kings are trapped, thanks to the forceful economy of White's play.

A particularly beautiful example of utilizing the same economical technique is seen in Diagram 23. The position finally forced by White is similar to the previous one, but it takes some smart finessing.

Diagram 23 (*White to play and win*)

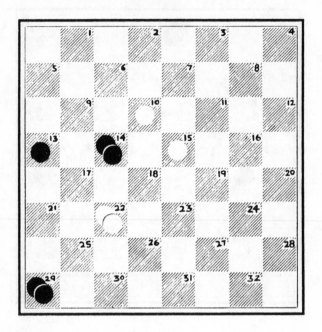

WHITE

White has blockaded the man on 13 and the King on 29. But White seems to be on the point of losing, for his man on 10 is attacked and White appears to have no saving move.

Thus, if 10—6, Black has the "breeches" attack . . . 14—10. And if White tries 10—7 in the position of Diagram 23, Black has the "breeches" attack . . . 14—18. What is White to do? He can win by an extremely subtle sacrifice.

BLACK	WHITE
....	22—26!!

Forcing Black to capture.

| 14—7 | 26—22! |

44 • **Winning Checker Tactics** •

Reestablishing the blockade. Although White is a King down, he must win.

7—3	15—11
13—17	....

An attempt to escape, but after White captures, he will still be able to trap the Black King now on 29.

....	22—13
20—25	13—17
25—21	17—22

White wins. Beautiful play, beginning with White's brilliant finesse 22—26!

Diagram 24 (*White to play and win*)

BLACK

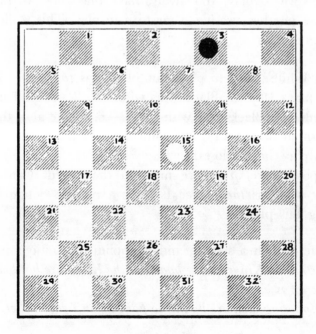

WHITE

Time and time again, it is important in the endgame to know who has *the move*—that is to say, it is important to know whether you can reach a position in which you control the last move, so that you can make a move that bottles up all your opponent's remaining men. Diagram 24 is a fundamental example.

White plays 15—11, winning at once, as Black's remaining man is trapped.

Hence we say that in Diagram 24, with White to play, he has *the move.* He controls the last move.

On the other hand, suppose that in Diagram 24 it were Black's turn to play. Then he would have *the move,* as he would play . . . 3—7, trapping White's last man.

From this you must not conclude, however, that because it is your turn to play, you always have *the move.* In fact, you may lose just because it *is* your turn to play. This is illustrated in Diagram 25.

It is White's turn to play, but Black has *the move.* Thus, if White plays 18—15, Black wins with . . . 2—7. And if White plays 18—14, Black wins with . . . 2—6. (Note also, that if in the position of Diagram 25 White's man is at 17 and it is his turn to play, he still loses!)

Suppose there are more men on the board. Can we see quickly who has *the move?* Is there a reliable system for calculating this play?

There is such a system, and it applies to positions in which
—*there are no Kings on the board or the Kings are bottled up*
—*material is even*
—*the opposing men are bound to fight against each other.*

Diagram 25 (*White to play*)

BLACK

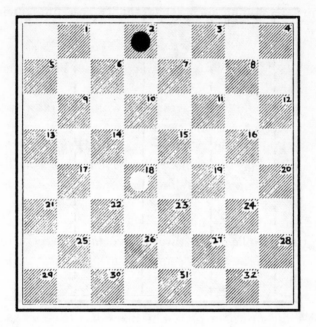

WHITE

(The last point means that if you have a Black man at 1 and a White man at 32, there is no point in calculating *the move,* as no problem of opposition need necessarily arise.)

Now to our system. At the beginning of the game, White's men on the row nearest him are placed on 29, 30, 31, and 32. If you draw imaginary lines through the vertical rows starting with these squares, as in Diagram 26, the four marked rows constitute "White's system."

Diagram 26 (*White's system*)

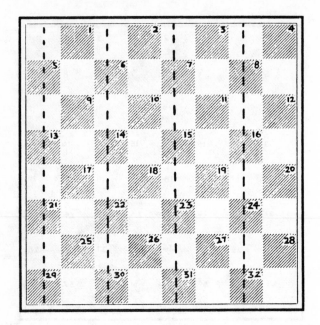

WHITE

Now let us see how this shapes up in the Black camp. At the beginning of the game Black's men nearest him are placed on 1, 2, 3, and 4. If you draw imaginary lines through the vertical rows starting with *these* squares, you get the set-up of Diagram 27.

Just as we have four vertical rows making up a group of squares we call "White's system," so the remaining four vertical rows make up a group of squares we call "Black's system."

Now, subject to the limitations mentioned on page 46, we can state these three rules: if it is your turn to play, and there

Diagram 27 (*Black's system*)

BLACK

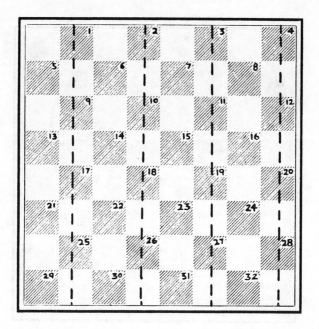

WHITE

is an *odd* number of men (of either color) in your system, you have *the move*. If it is your turn to play, and you have an *even* number of men in your system, your opponent has *the move*. If there are *no men* in your system, and it is your turn to play, your opponent has *the move*.

In Diagram 24, for example, it is White's turn to move, and he has one man in his system. Therefore White has *the move*, and he wins.

In Diagram 25 it is White's turn to move, and he has no men in his system. Therefore Black has *the move*, and *he* wins.

Now turn to Diagram 28, for a more complicated example of how to calculate *the move*.

Diagram 28 (*White to play and win*)

BLACK

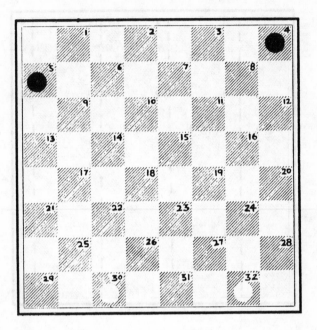

WHITE

Counting up, we find there are three men (two White and one Black) in the White system. Consequently, White has *the move* and will win—*if he makes the right first move.*

But how is he to determine which man to move first? To do this, White must be ready to put a man on 19 as soon as Black puts a man on 11. Also, White must be ready to put a man on 22 as soon as Black puts a man on 13 or 14.

But it takes White *two* moves to reach 22, while it takes him *three* moves to reach 19 from 32. Consequently his first move must be 32—28 or 32—27.

By comparing the right sequence with the wrong sequence,

we shall see why this distinction has to be made. First, the right sequence:

BLACK	WHITE
....	32—27!
4—8	....

Threatening . . . 8—11, so that White must play 27—24 or 27—23.

....	27—23

If now . . . 5—9 (threatening . . . 9—14), 30—25! (30—26 also wins); . . . 8—11, 23—19; . . . 9—14, 25—22 and White wins both Black men.

8—11	23—19
5—9	30—25
9—13	25—22

White wins.

Now for the wrong sequence (from Diagram 28):

BLACK	WHITE
....	30—25?
4—8!	32—27
8—11	....

If White now plays 27—23, Black reaches the King row by playing . . . 11—16 followed by . . . 16—20. White has spoiled his chances of winning.

....	27—24
11—15!	25—22

To stop . . . 15—18!

5—9	....

The position is a draw, as 24—20 is answered by . . . 15—19, and 22—17 by . . . 15—18.

In Diagram 29 White does not have *the move,* but by a dexterous maneuver he can get it and win easily.

Diagram 29 (*White to play and win*)

BLACK

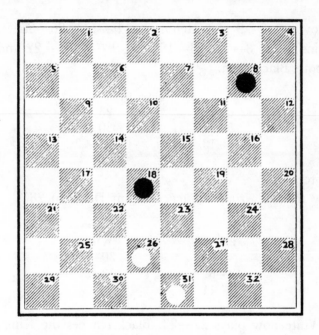

WHITE

It is White's turn to play, and there are two men (one White, one Black) in his system. Therefore Black has *the move.* But by offering an exchange, White can obtain *the move.*

BLACK	WHITE
....	26—23!
18—27	31—24

Now White has *the move* and wins.

8—11   24—19

White wins. This is still another example of the effective ways in which you can exploit the obligation to capture.

We conclude this chapter with a masterly display of checker tactics. At first sight Black ought to win easily, as he is ahead in material. Actually the win is difficult and requires a great deal of finesse.

Diagram 30 (*Black to play and win*)

BLACK

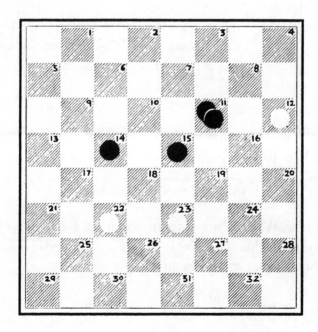

WHITE

• **Winning Checker Tactics** • 53

If it were White's turn to play, Black would win on the spot, as all of White's men would be lost. As matters stand, however, Black must give up the blockade.

BLACK	WHITE
11—16!	12—8

If now . . . 16—20?, 8—3(K)?; . . . 15—19!, 23—16; . . . 20—11 and Black wins.

However, on . . . 16—20? White plays 23—19! This draws after . . . 15—24, 8—3(K); . . . 24—27, 3—7; . . . 27—31(K), 7—10; 31—26; . . . 10—17 etc.

(Note that if . . . 15—19?—instead of . . . 16—20?—White draws with 22—18!)

16—12!	....

So that if White plays 8—3(K) there follows . . . 15—19!, 23—16; . . . 12—19 and Black traps White's King, for example 3—7; . . . 19—15, 7—2; . . . 15—10 and wins.

....	23—19!

White makes a determined effort to draw, the idea being . . . 12—3?, 19—10 and he gets a King by 10—6 etc.

15—24!	8—3(K)

Even now White is not without resources, for if . . . 24—27? (an unwary beginner's move), 3—7; . . . 27—31(K), 7—10 and White draws, as shown previously.

12—8!!	....

This exquisite move wins for Black.

....	3—12
24—27	12—16
27—31(K)	16—19
31—26	....

Black wins. A clever ending, with a great deal of finesse. Study this ending until you are thoroughly familiar with its subtle details.

In this chapter we have explained some of the basic elements of checker tactics—the two-for-one shot, the "breeches" attack, corner blocks, the value of *the move,* etc.

Repeatedly we have seen that the most plausible move is not always the best. A little thought, a little care, will often transform a seemingly barren position into a neat win. Checkers is a game in which economy of force pays special dividends.

3. Spectacular Traps in the Opening

Every checker player is thrilled by the opportunity to set off a brilliant multiple capture right in the opening. Such a capture generally leads to your getting an early King, and leaves your opponent demoralized and practically beaten at the very start.

But these traps are not only fun; they are eminently practical. Knowing them, you can make use of them repeatedly against weaker players; and, by the same token, you can avoid being trapped yourself.

The most valuable feature of these traps is the useful insight into correct opening play which they give you. They teach you to exercise caution and foresight in considering your opening moves. They demonstrate graphically the importance of solid opening formations. They also help you to become a good tactician, as you come to realize the lively possibilities so often buried in colorless-looking positions.

As you look at trap after trap, you must remember the moral that is constantly repeated: *these traps come about from the obligation to capture.* So, watch out for capturing possibilities!

(At the beginning of each trap we give the name of the opening in which it occurs. The openings are treated in detail in Chapter 4.)

BRISTOL CROSS

BLACK	WHITE
11—16	23—18

These moves form the opening.

16—20	24—19
8—11??	....

This natural-looking move leads to disaster (first pointed out by Canalejos, a Spanish player, about 1650!).

The right move for Black is . . . 10—14.

Diagram 31 (*White to play and win*)

BLACK

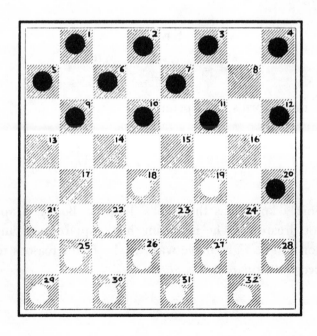

WHITE

A surprise sacrifice which leads to a series of winning exchanges.

10—19	18—14!

White is opening up the diagonal leading to 4.

9—18	22—8
4—11	27—24!

The point of the trap: White sets up a three-for-one shot.

20—27	31—8

White wins. He will be a whole King to the good after 8—4(K).

KELSO

BLACK	WHITE
10—15	....

This move forms the opening.

....	23—19
6—10	22—17
11—16??	....

Variously known as the Fool's Trap or Booby Trap. Black does not dream that he is leaving his 2 square in a vulnerable condition! (The right move was . . . 1—6, for reasons that will soon become apparent.)

Diagram 32 (*White to play and win*)

BLACK

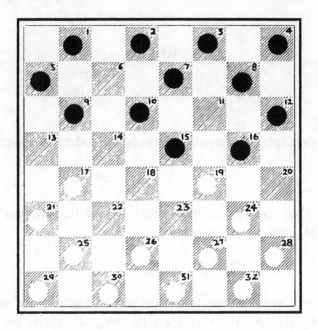

WHITE

....   17—13!

To force the disappearance of the man on 2.

16—23   13—6!

The other captures (27—11 or 26—19) would lose White his chances of carrying out the trap.

2—9   ....

Forced. But now the position is opened up for Black's three-for-one shot.

White wins. His material advantage is overwhelming.

KELSO

BLACK	WHITE
10—15	22—18
15—22	25—18

White captures *toward the center*—good on principle.

6—10	29—25

Playable—but White must bear in mind that he *may* become vulnerable on his 29 square.

10—15	....

With a nasty threat that can be satisfactorily defended by 18—14 (evading the threat on the long diagonal) or 26—22 (strengthening White's position on the long diagonal).

....	25—22??

Now Black can smash through to 25.

(See Diagram 33)

15—19!!	....

As in all these traps, the order of the moves is important. To win, Black must *first* play . . . 15—19!! and *then* . . . 9—14! in due course.

....	23—16

60 • Spectacular Traps in the Opening •

Diagram 33 (*Black to play and win*)

BLACK

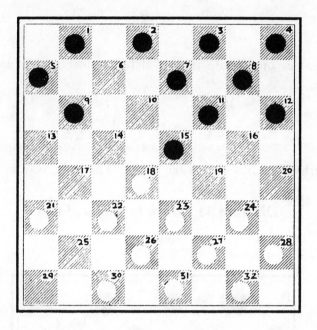

WHITE

———

If White plays 24—15 Black wins with . . . 9—14! as in the text continuation.

12—19   24—15

Now Black has the position he wants. He forces White to open up the enfeebled diagonal with:

9—14!   18—9
11—25   ....

Black wins. He will win the man on 9 and then get a King with . . . 25—29(K).

BLACK	WHITE
10—15	23—18
12—16	26—23
8—12	30—26

Playable, but White must watch out for trouble on his 30 square.

16—20	21—17
9—13	17—14
6—9	23—19??

Overlooking Black's master stroke. The right way is 24—19.

Diagram 34 (*Black to play and win*)

BLACK

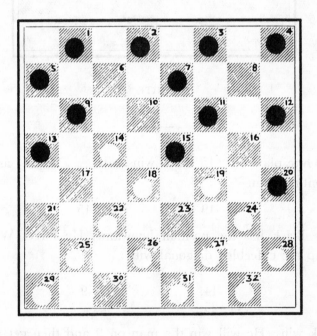

WHITE

This sacrifice is aimed at White's 30 square. Thus, if White plays 19—10 Black replies with the deadly . . . 17—21 and White is helpless.

....	22—6
1—17	19—10

This forced capture lays White open to a catastrophe.

7—30(K)	......

Black wins. He has an overwhelming material advantage.

KELSO

BLACK	WHITE
10—15	21—17
11—16	17—13
16—20	25—21
8—11	29—25
4—8	......

After this, the 4 square *may* become vulnerable.

......	22—17
7—10	25—22
9—14	24—19
15—24	28—19

Now the right play for Black is . . . 11—15 etc.

11—16??	......

Diagram 35 (*White to play and win*)

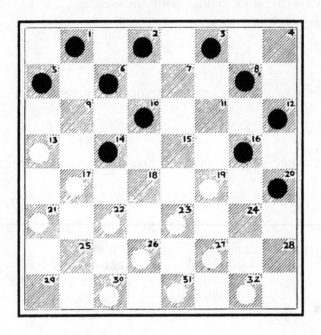

Now White is in position to triumph on the long diagonal by a series of smart exchanges.

....	19—15!!
10—19	17—10
6—15	13—9!

This second sacrifice is the real point.

5—14	23—18!
14—23	27—4(K)

White wins. His King will have decisive effect.

64 • Spectacular Traps in the Opening •

DENNY

BLACK	WHITE
10—14	....

This move forms the opening.

....	23—19
11—16	26—23
9—13	....

Now White can play 22—18 or 22—17 with a satisfactory game.

....	24—20??

Diagram 36 (*Black to play and win*)

BLACK

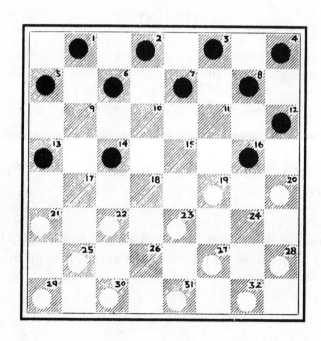

WHITE

As a result of White's last move, his obligation to capture will soon prove ruinous for him.

14—17!!	21—14

Or 20—11; . . . 17—26, 31—22 and White's position is opened up for the murderous shot . . . 8—31 (K).

6—10!	20—11

Must.

10—26	31—22
8—31 (K)	....

Black wins. He has an overwhelming material advantage.

DENNY

BLACK	WHITE
10—14	24—19
11—16	28—24
16—20	19—15
9—13	23—19
7—10	32—28
14—18	....

Now White's best is 26—23, after which . . . 2—7 leads to exchanges.

....	21—17??

By a series of brilliant moves, Black will now reach 31. Note that his moves must be played in the exact order given.

Diagram 37 (*Black to play and win*)

BLACK

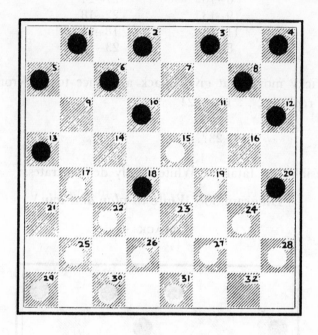

WHITE

10—14!!	17—10
13—17!	22—13
18—23!	27—18
20—27	31—24
8—11!	....

Breaking up White's formation.

....	15—8
6—31(K)	....

Black wins. He will win the man on 8, and he has a King.

BLACK	WHITE
10—14	24—19
6—10	27—24
9—13	22—18
11—15	18—11
8—15	23—18!

A tricky move that gives Black a chance to go wrong. His proper reply is . . . 15—22!

14—23?? ....

Plausible but fatal, as White neatly demonstrates.

Diagram 38 (*White to play and win*)

BLACK

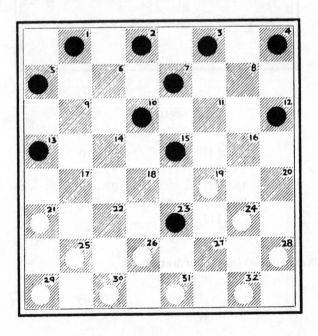

WHITE

| | 19—16!! |
| 12—19 | 21—17! |

First White sacrificed in the center, then on the right wing and now on the left wing. Remarkably imaginative play!

13—22	25—11
7—16	24—6
1—10	26—12

Black wins. His sacrifices have netted him a man to the good.

DENNY

BLACK	WHITE
10—14	22—18
11—16	25—22
16—20	24—19
8—11	19—15
4—8	22—17
12—16	....

Here . . . 9—13 leads to a more solid formation for Black.

....	17—10
7—14	29—25
3—7??	....

Instead, . . . 2—7 would have avoided the following remarkable shot.

(See Diagram 39)

Diagram 39 (*White to play and win*)

BLACK

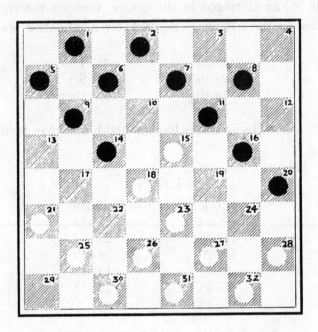

WHITE

....   15—10!!

This startling sacrifice allows Black to win three men and get a King—and yet White wins.

6—29(K)   30—25!

Now we see the reason for White's generosity.

29—22   26—3(K)
8—12   3—8

White wins. His King will prove too strong for the Black men.

CROSS

BLACK	WHITE
11—15	23—18

These moves form the opening.

8—11	27—23
10—14	24—20
6—10	28—24
3—8	23—19??

This proves disastrous, as it commits White to a later capture that will be ruinous for him.

Diagram 40 (*Black to play and win*)

BLACK

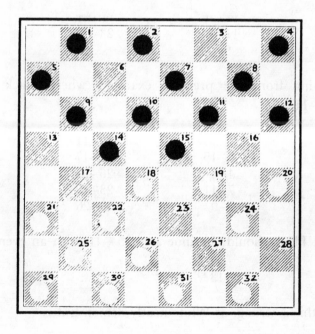

WHITE

White expects to recover his man without complications, but Black has a surprise reply.

15—18!!	22—6
1—10	27—18

Now Black plays a move that forces a three-for-one shot.

11—16!	20—11
8—31(K)	....

Black wins. His King will have a decisive effect.

CROSS

BLACK	WHITE
11—15	23—18
9—14	....

Varying from the previous example, where Black played . . . 8—11.

....	18—11
8—15	22—17
4—8	26—23
7—11	23—19
5—9	30—26

Now Black should continue . . . 15—18 with an even game.

9—13??	....

But this is wrong, as White neatly demonstrates.

Diagram 41 (*White to play and win*)

BLACK

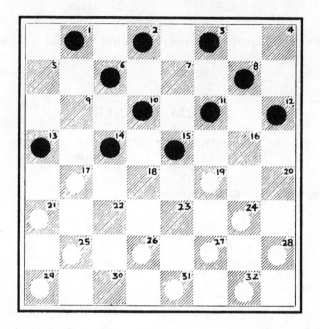

WHITE

As so often happens in these traps, a mistake on one wing is punished by a surprise reply on the other wing. The effect is to produce an over-all weakening in the victim's formation.

....	19—16!!

If Black now plays . . . 11—20, there follows 26—23; . . . 13—22, 25—4(K) and wins.

12—19	27—23!

This creates the setting for a different kind of three-for-one shot.

13—22	23—7
2—11	25—2 (K)

White wins. He has an overwhelming material advantage.

SINGLE CORNER

BLACK	WHITE
11—15	22—18

These moves form the opening.

15—22	25—18
8—11	29—25
4—8	25—22
10—15	24—20

White threatens to win with 20—16! Black parries with a trap of his own.

12—16	....

Now the right reply for White is 21—17.

....	27—24??

An insidious move which threatens a two-for-one shot by 24—19 etc. However, the refutation of this move goes back to at least 1756. (28—24?? loses in the same way.)

White has stumbled into the trap variously known as "the Old Farmer" and "the Goose Walk."

Diagram 42 (*Black to play and win*)

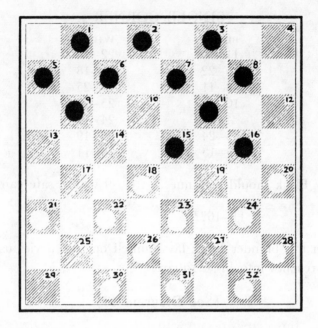

WHITE

15—19!!	....

Another way to work the same trap is . . . 16—19!!, 23—16; . . . 15—19!, 24—15; and now . . . 9—14! leads to the same position.

....	24—15
16—19!	23—16
9—14!	....

Smashing White's formation on the long diagonal.

....	18—9
11—25	....

Black wins. He picks up the unprotected man on 9 and then proceeds to get a King with . . . 25—29(K).

SINGLE CORNER

BLACK	WHITE
11—15	22—18
15—22	25—18
8—11	29—25
10—15	25—22
4—8	24—19
15—24	28—19
9—13	18—14

Now Black should continue . . . 6—9 with a safe game.

      11—16??   ....

With this blunder Black lays himself open to a vicious attack which reaches into his 4 square.

(See Diagram 43)

Note that here too White answers a mistake on one side of the board with a surprise reply in an apparently remote sector.

      ....   14—10!!

Giving Black the opportunity for . . . 6—24, 27—4(K). Black squirms, but ultimately he is forced into the capture.

7—14	22—17!
13—22	26—10

Thus Black is forced to bite into the sour apple.

      6—24   27—4(K)

Black wins. With a King to the good, he naturally has an easy win.

Diagram 43 (*White to play and win*)

BLACK

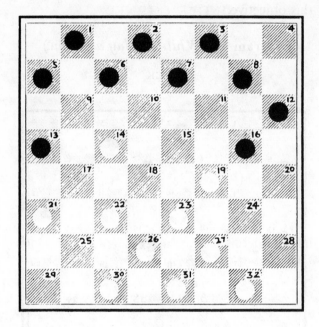

WHITE

SINGLE CORNER

BLACK	WHITE
11—15	22—18
15—22	25—18
8—11	24—19
10—15	19—10
6—22	26—17
9—13	17—14
11—15	28—24

Black's safe course is now . . . 1—6—or even . . . 15—18.

4—8?? ....

• **Spectacular Traps in the Opening** • 77

But this is all wrong, as it creates a vulnerable formation on the long diagonal. White's job is now to play 23—18 in such a way that Black cannot stop the double jump. Watch how White achieves this objective.

Diagram 44 (*White to play and win*)

BLACK

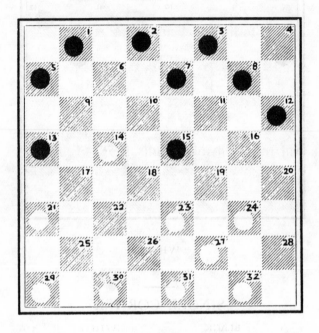

WHITE

....	21—17!!

The first step.

13—22	14—10!
7—14	23—18!

Now he can play it.

14—23	27—4(K)

White wins. He continues 30—25 followed by 25—18 and with the help of his extra King he has an easy win.

BRISTOL

BLACK	WHITE
11—16	24—20

These moves form the opening.

16—19	23—16
12—19	22—18
8—11	27—23
4—8	....

Black will regain his man with . . . 8—12.

....	23—16
8—12	32—27
12—19	27—23

Now Black can maintain equality with . . . 11—16, 20—11; . . . 7—16 etc.

3—8??	....

Black plans on answering 23—16 with . . . 8—12 as he did previously. But here he critically weakens his King row, as White demonstrates incisively by a series of brilliant moves.

(See Diagram 45)

....	23—16
8—12	....

So far so good.

....	21—17!!

Diagram 45 (*White to play and win*)

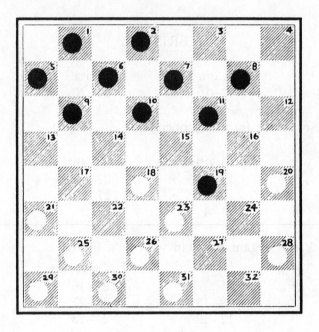

WHITE

———

Preparing the following stroke.

12—19	18—14!!
9—18	26—23!
18—27	....

Or . . . 19—26, 31—8 with the same effect.

....	31—8

White wins. He has a decisive material advantage and is about to reach the King row.

80 • Spectacular Traps in the Opening •

In these traps you have seen how it is possible to win quickly and brilliantly when your opponent overlooks the possibility that forced captures can lead to instant ruin. Thus these traps stress the need for constant vigilance and foresight.

Another valuable feature of these traps is that they form a natural introduction to the study of opening play. Not only do they teach you the importance of careful planning; they also emphasize the need for solid formations and due attention to the vulnerable state of the King row. Thus, by stressing a blend of strategy and tactics, they lead us to a study of the principal checker openings.

4. How to Get a Good Game in the Opening

In the spectacular traps of the previous chapter, you saw how easy it is to go wrong in the opening. Before the unwary victim quite realizes what has happened, he has a lost game.

It is therefore useful to familiarize yourself with the most important recommended lines of play, so that you can get off to a good start. And in addition, if your opponent adopts inferior lines, you will be able to take advantage of his lapses.

The inexperienced player may well be baffled when he starts a game. He has a choice of seven different opening moves; his opponent has a choice of replies to each one. Some are good, some bad, some colorless. How is he to know which is which?

To know all the openings, in all their intricacies, is the job of the expert. He must know every little fine point. For the average player the problem is less critical. A knowledge of the over-all picture will eliminate much of the initial confusion. Then he can experiment with different openings, and decide which he prefers. Eventually, he will specialize and deepen his knowledge. But, at the start it is better to develop a general idea of the whole opening repertoire.

We turn now to the seven opening groups which stem from White's first move.

The following table lists Black's possible first moves in the order of merit:

Best	...11—15
Second-best	... 9—14
Third and fourth-best	...11—16
or	...10—15
Fifth-best	...10—14
Sixth-best	...12—16
Seventh-best	... 9—13

A word of caution about this listing. It does not follow that if you adopt the better opening moves you will necessarily win—or that if you adopt the inferior opening moves you will necessarily lose.

Long experience with these opening moves has shown that if you start off with the better moves, you are more likely to have the initiative, more likely to build up an aggressive formation, more likely to come off unscathed with a draw if you play second-best moves. On the other hand, if you start with the inferior opening moves, you may find yourself on the defensive in short order; you may reach positions in which only first-rate skill will make a draw possible.

... 9—13 (EDINBURGH) GROUP

This is considered Black's weakest first move, as it moves a man to the side of the board and allows White to take the initiative in the center, where the men have the greatest mobility.

White has good replies in 22—18! and 24—19! while 21—17? (the Switcher) is comparatively weak and gives Black fine prospects.

BLACK	WHITE
9–13	22–18!

Another good line of play for White is 24—19!; . . . 11—15, 28—24; . . . 6—9, 22—18 etc.

White has a number of other moves for an even game; for example:

I   . . . 9—13, 22—17; . . . 13—22, 25—18; . . . 11—15, 18—11; . . . 8—15, 21—17 etc.

II   . . . 9—13, 23—18; . . . 12—16, 18—14; . . . 10—17, 21—14; . . . 6—10, 24—20; . . . 10—17, 25—21 etc.

III   . . . 9—13, 23—19; . . . 11—15, 22—18; . . . 15—22, 25—18; . . . 10—14, 18—9; . . . 5—14, 27—23 etc.

IV   . . . 9—13, 24—20; . . . 11—15, 22—17; . . . 13—22, 25—11; . . . 8—15, 21—17; . . . 5—9, 17—13 etc.

Diagram 46 (*Black to play*)

BLACK

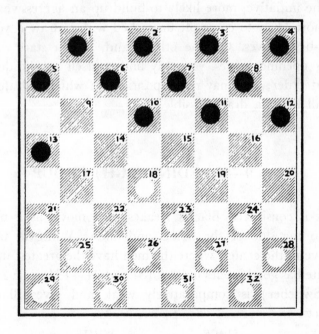

WHITE

$$12-16 \qquad \ldots\ldots$$

Generally considered Black's best continuation.

....	24—20
8—12	25—22
10—15	18—14
16—19	23—16
12—19	14—10!

Leads to interesting play.

7—14	27—23

Diagram 47 (*Black to play*)

BLACK

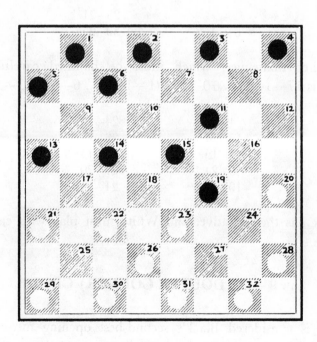

WHITE

Black is safe if he continues . . . 14—18!, 23—7; . . . 18—25, 29—22; . . . 2—11. On the other hand (see Diagram 47) . . . 2—7?, 23—16; . . . 6—10, 30—25 etc. leads to an untenable position for Black.

SWITCHER

BLACK	WHITE
9—13	21—17?

White's weakest reply.

11—15!	....

This gives Black a strong game. (This opening also comes about after . . . 11—15, 21—17?; . . . 9—13 etc.)

....	25—21
8—11	30—25

Another maneuver, which must be handled carefully by White, is 17—14; . . . 10—17, 21—14; . . . 6—10, 22—17 etc.

4—8	24—19
15—24	28—19
11—15	17—14
15—24	27—20
10—17	21—14

Black has the initiative, and White must play with care.

. . . 9—14 (DOUBLE CORNER) GROUP

This is considered Black's second-best opening move. Note that (unlike . . . 9—13) this is a move toward the center, and it is therefore good on principle.

As for White's replies, 22—17! and 22—18! are best, while 23—19 and 24—20 are playable. Black gets a strong game after 23—18 (Double Cross) and after 24—19.

BLACK	WHITE
9—14	22—18!

Here 23—18 (the Double Cross); . . . 14—23, 27—18; . . . 12—16, 18—14; . . . 10—17, 21—14; . . . 6—9 is good for Black.

Similarly, after 24—19; . . . 11—15, 22—18; . . . 15—24, 18—9; . . . 5—14, 28—19; . . . 8—11 Black has some initiative.

On the other hand, after 24—20; . . . 5—9!, 22—18!; . . . 11—16, 20—11; . . . 8—22, 25—18 the game is even.

5—9	24—20
11—16	20—11
8—22	25—18
4—8	28—24
8—11	24—19
11—16	29—25
7—11	....

(See Diagram 48)

Now White plays a well-timed thrust which relieves his position.

....	18—15!
11—18	21—17
14—21	23—5
16—23	26—19

The freeing exchanges have assured White of equality.

Diagram 48 (*White to play*)

BLACK

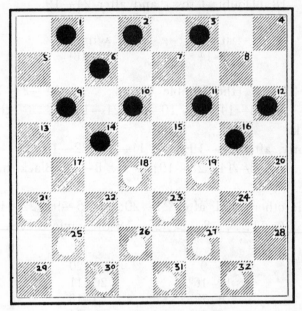

WHITE

———

PIONEER

BLACK	WHITE
9—14	22—17!
11—16	....

This forms the Pioneer Opening, a very popular line of play.
(Black is better off with . . . 11—15, 25—22; . . . 15—19, 24—15;
. . . 10—19, 23—16; . . . 12—19, 17—10; . . . 6—15 etc.)

....	25—22
8—11	22—18
16—20	18—9
5—14	29—25
11—15	....

Black's best.

....	25—22
7—11	17—13

Diagram 49 (*Black to play*)

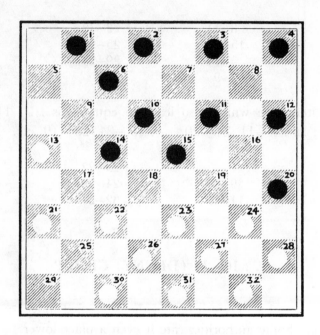

While the game will be even with the best play, Black must proceed with care.

4—8	22—17
15—18	24—19
18—22	19—16
12—19	23—7
2—11	26—23

Even game.

DEFIANCE

BLACK	WHITE
9—14	23—19
11—15	27—23

These moves form the opening, which leads to interesting battles, as its name indicates.

BLACK	WHITE
8—11	22—18
15—22	25—9
5—14	29—25
6—9	....

An alternative which also leads to equality is . . . 11—15, 25—22; . . . 7—11, 24—20; . . . 15—24, 28—19, etc.

BLACK	WHITE
....	25—22
9—13	24—20
11—15	32—27

. . . 10—14 (DENNY) GROUP

This is rated as the fifth best of the seven first moves available to Black. (Some authorities rate it even a place lower.)

White does very well with 22—17! or 23—19! or 24—19! for his first move, while 23—18 and 24—20 are weak first moves for White that give Black good prospects.

VARIATION I

BLACK	WHITE
10—14	....

This move gives the opening its name.

....	22—17!

Note that after 23—18; . . . 14—23, 27—18; . . . 12—16, 32—27; . . . 16—20, 26—23; . . . 6—10, 30—26; . . . 11—15 Black has excellent prospects.

Similarly, 10—14, 24—20; . . . 11—15 is a good formation for Black.

7—10	17—13
3—7	25—22

White also gets a good game with 24—20.

14—17	21—14
9—25	29—22

Diagram 50 (*Black to play*)

BLACK

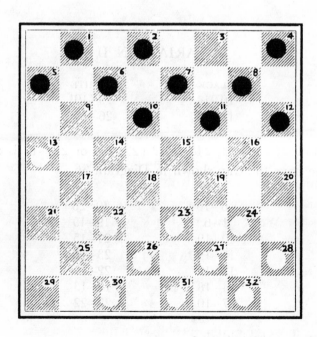

WHITE

Here . . . 10—14 is a bit on the risky side, as may be seen from the continuation 24—19; . . . 6—10, 22—18; . . . 14—17, 27—24; . . . 1—6, 19—15; . . . 10—19, 24—15; . . . 12—16? (. . . 6—9! draws). Now White wins brilliantly by 15—10!!; . . . 6—22, 13—9!; . . . 5—14, 23—18; . . . 14—23, 26—3(K), etc.

11—15	....

The safest play.

....	24—20
7—11	23—18
12—16	27—23

White has the initiative.

VARIATION II

BLACK	WHITE
10—14	23—19!
11—16	26—23

If now . . . 9—13, 24—20?? (22—18 or 22—17 is correct) and we have the trap shown in Diagram 36.

6—10	30—26
1—6	19—15
10—19	24—15
16—19	23—16
12—19	22—17
14—18	17—13
7—10	25—22

White has the initiative.

VARIATION III

10—14

WHITE
24—19!

And now . . . 11—16, 28—24 may lead to the trap shown
in Diagram 37.

6—10 ....

A good line for White here is 27—24; . . . 9—13, 22—18;
. . . 11—15, 18—11; . . . 8—15, 23—18 and now . . . 15—22!
is best for Black—not . . . 14—23?? leading to the trap shown
in Diagram 38.

.... 22—17

Diagram 51 (*Black to play*)

BLACK

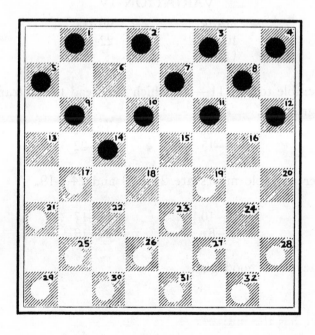

WHITE

Or . . . 9—13, 28—24; . . . 13—22, 25—9; . . . 5—14, 26—22 and White retains the initiative.

....   17—13

A reasonable alternative is 26—22; . . . 15—24, 28—19; . . 7—11!, 17—13 with a good game for White.

15—24	13—6
2—9	28—19

White has the initiative.

VARIATION IV

BLACK	WHITE
10—14	22—18
11—15	....

Preferable to . . . 11—16, which may lead to the trap shown in Diagram 39.

....	18—11
8—15	26—22

Other playable moves are 24—20 and 24—19.

6—10	22—17
4—8	23—19

White has a good game.

This move ranks with . . . 11—16 as Black's third-best opening move. White's best replies are 21—17! or 22—17! or 22—18!—all of which give him an excellent game. On the other hand, 24—19 and 24—20 are comparatively weak replies.

VARIATION I

BLACK	WHITE
10—15	21—17!

An even game results from 23—18; . . . 12—16, 26—23; . . . 16—19 (. . . 8—12 may lead to the trap shown in Diagram 34), 23—16; . . . 11—20, 18—11; . . . 8—15, 22—18 etc.

11—16	....

If . . . 9—13?, 17—14; . . . 11—16, 24—19; . . . 15—24, 28—19; . . . 6—9, 22—18 and Black has to fight for the draw.

....	17—13

Here 24—20 is a promising alternative.

(See Diagram 52)

16—20	....

Instead, . . . 8—11? is much weaker because of . . . 24—20! and it is questionable whether Black can hold the position.

....	25—21
8—11	24—19

White can also try 29—25 which may lead to the trap shown in Diagram 35.

Diagram 52 (*Black to play*)

BLACK

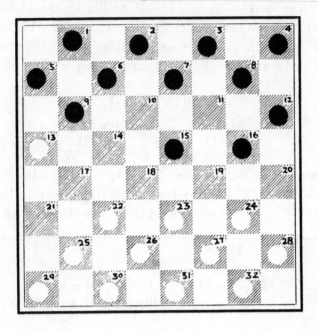

WHITE

15—24	28—19
11—16	22—18
7—10	26—22

White has the initiative.

VARIATION II

BLACK	WHITE
10—15	22—17!
11—16	23—19

An enterprising move.

16—23	26—10
6—15	17—13
9—14	25—22
12—16	27—23
8—12	24—19
15—24	28—19

White has the edge. Black must play carefully to draw.

VARIATION III

10—15	22—18!
15—22	25—18
6—10	....

Diagram 53 (*White to play*)

BLACK

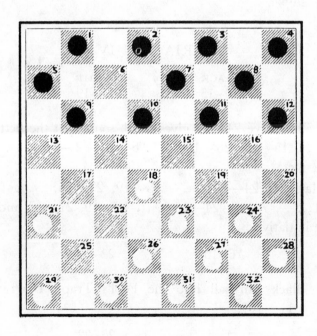

WHITE

A playable alternative is . . . 11—15, 18—11; . . . 8—15 and now 26—22; . . . 4—8, 24—19; . . . 15—24, 28—19; . . . 8—11, 22—18; . . . 6—10, 29—25; . . . 2—6 (threatens . . . 10—15! with a three-for-one shot), 25—22 (defends the threat) and White has a good game.

....	29—25
11—15	....

Here . . . 10—15 gives White a chance to fall into a diabolical trap with 25—22?? (see Diagram 33).

....	18—11
8—15	25—22
4—8	21—17
9—13	23—18

Even game.

VARIATION IV

BLACK	WHITE
10—15	23—19

The alternative 24—19 gives Black somewhat the better of it after . . . 15—24, 28—19; . . . 6—10, 22—17; . . . 9—14, 25—22 etc.

Similarly, if 24—20; . . . 15—19, 23—16; . . . 12—19, 27—24; . . . 7—10, 24—15; . . . 10—19, 21—17 and Black has the initiative.

6—10	22—17

Now Black can fall into the Fool's Trap (Diagram 32) with . . . 11—16??

1—6	25—22
11—16	17—13

A good alternative is 29—25.

16—23	26—19

Even game.

. . . 11—15 GROUP

This thrust at the center is considered Black's best opening move. It is so popular that it has branched off into more openings than any other initial move. Among the replies that can be recommended for White are 23—19 or 23—18 or 22—18 or 22—17. On the other hand, 24—20 and 24—19 and 21—17 are all considered inferior in varying degrees.

A useful point for the beginner to know is that after . . . 11—15, 21—17 Black can play the favorable Switcher (page 86) by continuing . . . 9—13 etc.

GLASGOW

BLACK	WHITE
11—15	23—19!
8—11	22—17
11—16	....

These moves form the opening, which is an excellent one for inexperienced players to adopt.

Instead of his last move, Black can select the picturesquely named Laird and Lady opening, which goes . . . 9—13, 17—14; . . . 10—17, 21—14 and leads to lively play.

....	24—20
16—23	27—11
7—16	20—11
3—7	28—24

The alternative 11—8 is also playable.

7—16	24—20
16—19	25—22
4—8	29—25

Diagram 54 (*Black to play*)

BLACK

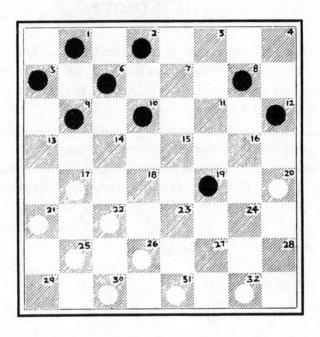

WHITE

19—24   ....

This leads to interesting complications. If now 32—28; . . .
8—11, 28—19; . . . 11—15, 20—16; . . . 15—24, 16—11 etc.

....   17—14

An interesting though only temporary sacrifice. Instead, White can play safe with 17—13; . . . 9—14, 26—23 etc.

9—18	22—15
10—19	32—28
6—10!	....

So that if White plays 26—23 there follows . . . 19—26, 30—23; . . . 8—11, 28—19; . . . 11—15 and wins.

....	25—22

If now . . . 8—11, 22—18 (to stop . . . 11—15) with an interesting draw by . . . 5—9, 21—17; . . . 10—15, 26—23; . . . 19—26, 28—10; . . . 2—6, 31—22; . . . 6—15 etc.

5—9	22—18

(See Diagram 55)

If now . . . 8—11 White plays 21—17 and holds the position despite the fact that he is temporarily a man down.

Black therefore "pitches" a man, and this leads to interesting complications.

9—14	18—9
1—5	9—6
2—9	20—16
9—14	26—23

The safest, at last recovering the sacrificed man.

19—26	28—19
5—9	31—22

Even game.

Diagram 55 (*Black to play*)

BLACK

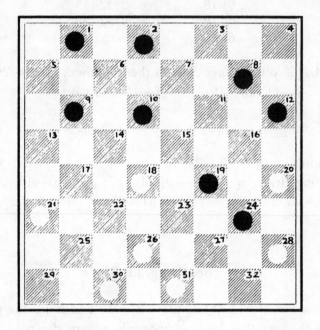

WHITE

OLD FOURTEENTH

BLACK	WHITE
11—15	23—19!
8—11	22—17
4—8	....

These moves form the opening, which also has many interesting possibilities. Instead, ... 3—8 forms the intricate Almà opening, for example 25—22; ... 11—16, 27—23; ... 7—11, 24—20, etc.

....	17—13
15—18	24—20

If now . . . 9—14, 28—24; . . . 10—15, 19—10; . . . 6—15, 26—23 Black should continue . . . 15—19!, 24—15; . . . 5—9!, 13—6; . . . 1—26, 31—15; . . . 11—18 with equality (but not . . . 12—16?, 23—19!; . . . 16—23, 20—16!; . . . 11—20, 25—22; . . . 18—25, 27—4(K) and White wins).

11—15	28—24
8—11	26—23
9—14	31—26

Not 30—26?, when Black replies . . . 6—9! forcing White into an untenable position.

| 6—9 | 13—6 |
| 2—9 | 26—22 |

Diagram 56 (*Black to play*)

BLACK

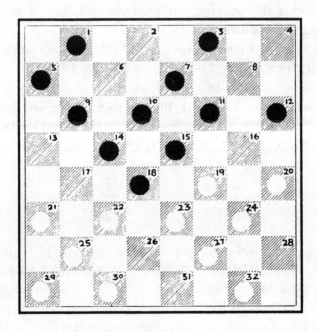

WHITE

If Black now plays the plausible . . . 9—13??, he loses by one
of the most spectacular shots known on the checkerboard: 20—
16!!; . . . 11—20, 22—17!; . . . 13—22, 21—17!; . . . 14—21,
23—14; . . . 10—17, 25—2(K) etc.

1—6	22—17
18—22	25—18
15—22	....

Even game.

SOUTER

BLACK	WHITE
11—15	23—19!
9—14	22—17
6—9	....

This forms the opening, an old-fashioned line of play with
interesting possibilities.

With . . . 5—9 instead, we get the Fife, another ancient but
lively line, for example 17—13; . . . 14—18, 19—16; . . . 12—
19, 26—23; . . . 19—26, 30—5, etc.

And with . . . 7—11 at Black's third move we have the
Whilter, which may go as follows: 25—22; . . . 11—16, 26—
23; . . . 5—9, 17—13; . . . 3—7, 29—25, etc.

....	17—13
2—6	26—22
8—11	22—17

If Black now plays . . . 4—8?? he weakens his game irre-
trievably. There follows: 27—23; . . . 15—18, 32—27; . . .
11—15, 30—26; . . . 8—11, 26—22; . . . 3—8, 31—26; . . .
11—16, and now White wins brilliantly with 24—20!!; . . .
15—31(K), 22—15; . . . 31—22, 20—2(K); . . . 10—26,
17—10!; . . . 6—15, 13—6; . . . 1—10, 25—4(K) etc.

Diagram 57 (*Black to play*)

BLACK

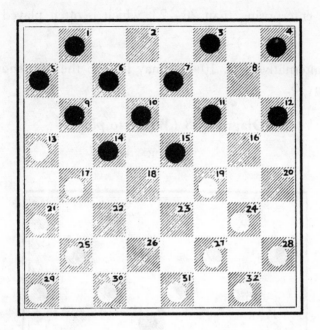

WHITE

14—18	25—22
18—25	29—22

Even game.

CROSS

BLACK	WHITE
11—15	23—18

These moves form the opening. White gets excellent counter-attacking chances.

8—11	....

Also playable is . . . 9—14, which may lead to the trap shown in Diagram 41.

....   27—23

More enterprising than 26—23, which is often played here.

4—8   ....

The alternative . . . 10—14 may lead to the trap shown in Diagram 40.

Diagram 58 (*White to play*)

BLACK

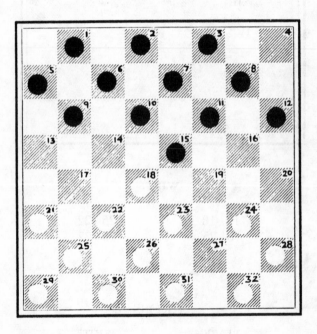

WHITE

Here White can set a trap and play 24—20, hoping for . . . 9—13?? (. . . 15—19! is correct), 20—16!; . . . 12—19, 23—16; . . . 11—20, 18—4(K) and wins.

106 • How to Get a Good Game in the Opening •

	23—19
10—14	19—10
14—23	26—19
7—14	24—20
6—10	22—17
9—13	30—26

After simplifying exchanges (. . . 13—22, 25—9; . . . 5—14 etc.) the game is even.

SINGLE CORNER

BLACK	WHITE
11—15	22—18

These moves form the opening, which gives Black a slight initiative—though White possesses ample resources.

15—22	25—18
12—16	

Here . . . 8—11 may lead to the traps pictured in Diagrams 42, 43, and 44.

	29—25

More conservative than 18—14, which is also playable.

10—14	25—22
16—20	24—19
6—10	

Or . . . 8—11, 19—16; . . . 4—8, 28—24; . . . 6—10, 16—12 with level chances.

	22—17

Even game.

• **How to Get a Good Game in the Opening** • 107

BLACK	WHITE
11—15	22—17
15—19	....

These moves form the opening.

If instead of . . . 15—19 Black plays . . . 8—11, then after 17—13; . . . 15—18 we have the Maid of the Mill, with even prospects after 23—14; . . . 9—18, 26—23; . . . 10—14, 24—20 etc.

....	24—15
10—19	23—16·
12—19	25—22

Diagram 59 (*Black to play*)

BLACK

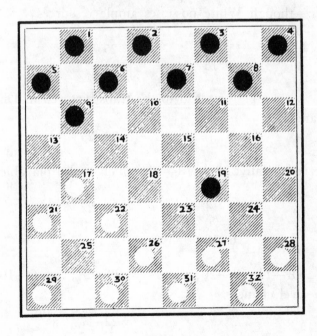

WHITE

At this point Black can play . . . 9—14, 17—10; . . . 6—15, 21—17; . . . 5—9, 17—13; . . . 2—6, 30—25; . . . 7—10 (but not . . . 9—14??, 26—23!; . . . 19—26, 22—18!; . . . 15—22, 25—2(K) and White wins).

8—11	27—23

If White plays 29—25 instead, he will find himself in serious trouble after . . . 11—15. In that case . . . 17—13! holds the position, whereas 27—23?? loses by . . . 9—13!, 23—16; . . . 15—18!, 22—15; . . . 13—29(K) etc.

4—8	23—16
11—20	22—18
8—11	32—27

The position is even.

AYRSHIRE LASSIE

BLACK	WHITE
11—15	24—20

These moves form the opening.

White's first move here is slightly inferior, as is also 24—19 (the Second Double Corner) with the likely continuation . . . 15—24, 28—19; . . . 8—11, 22—18; . . . 9—14, 18—9; . . . 5—14, 25—22 etc.

8—11	28—24
4—8	23—19

Now Black must avoid . . . 9—13?? for then White wins with 20—16!!; . . . 11—20, 22—17; . . . 13—22, 25—4(K).

15—18	22—15
11—18	26—22
7—11	22—15
11—18	30—26
8—11	....

Diagram 60 (*White to play*)

BLACK

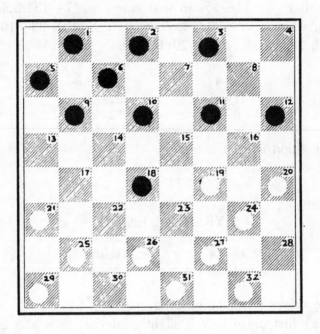

WHITE

Here White can go grievously wrong with 26—22?? allowing
Black to win with . . . 11—16!!, 20—11; . . . 3—7!, 22—15;
. . . 7—23, 27—18; . . . 10—28, etc.

....	25—22
18—25	29—22
11—15	27—23

Black has a slight initiative.

... 11—16 (BRISTOL) GROUP

Together with . . . 9—14, this ranks as Black's third-best opening move. The best replies are 22—18 or 24—19, while 23—19? should definitely be avoided by White.

BRISTOL

BLACK	WHITE
11—16	24—20

After 22—17; . . . 16—19, 23—16; . . . 12—19, 24—15; 10—19, 25—22 Black has a slight initiative.

Or White can play 21—17; . . . 9—13, 25—21; . . . 5—9, 23—18; . . . 10—15, 18—11; . . . 8—15 with about an éven game.

16—19	23—16
12—19	22—18

If Black now plays . . . 8—11 we may get the trap shown in Diagram 45.

9—14	18—9
5—14	25—22
10—15	22—17
7—10	20—16
2—7	30—25

Even game.

BRISTOL CROSS

BLACK	WHITE
11—16	23—18

These moves form the opening.

16—20	24—19

Note that . . . 8—11?? in reply would now be a gross blunder (Diagram 31).

A good alternative is 26—23; . . . 8—11, 22—17; . . . 7—10, 30—26 etc.

7—10	22—17
9—13	27—23
13—22	25—9
5—14	29—25

White has a slight initiative.

MILLBURY

BLACK	WHITE
11—16	22—18
8—11	....

Better than . . . 16—19, 24—15; . . . 10—19, 23—16; . . . 12—19, 25—22 etc.

....	25—22
16—20	22—17

This gives White more play than 29—25; . . . 10—14, 18—15; . . . 11—18, 22—15; . . . 9—13, 24—19 etc.

9—14	18—9
5—14	29—25
11—15	25—22
7—11	17—13

White has a slight initiative.

PAISLEY

BLACK	WHITE
11—16	24—19

These moves form the opening.

8—11	22—18
10—14	....

Or . . . 4—8, 18—14; . . . 9—18, 23—14; . . . 10—17, 21—14; . . . 16—23, 27—18; . . . 12—16, 28—24 with slightly better chances for White.

....	25—22

Here 26—22; . . . 16—20, 22—17; . . . 7—10, 30—26; . . . 11—16, 26—22; . . . 9—13, 18—9; . . . 5—14, 22—18 is a good alternative for White.

4—8	27—24

And here too White can vary satisfactorily with 22—17; . . . 9—13, 18—9; . . . 13—22, 26—17; . . . 6—22, 30—26 etc.

16—20	31—27
6—10	19—16

White has a slight initiative.

. . . 12—16 (DUNDEE) GROUP

This is a comparatively weak move and is considered the sixth-best of Black's seven possible opening moves. White's best reply is 24—20; of the alternatives, only 23—19? is bad enough to be unplayable.

DUNDEE

BLACK	WHITE
12—16	24—20

Best; White establishes a strong grip on the side square. Other White moves are less pressing. For example, 24—19 allows Black to improve his chances by transposing into the Paisley with . . . 8—12.

After . . . 12—16, 22—18; . . . 16—20, 25—22; . . . 8—12, 22—17; . . . 9—14, 18—9; . . . 5—14, 29—25 or . . . 12—16, 23—18; . . . 16—20, 24—19; . . . 11—15, 18—11; . . . 8—24, 28—19 White has a slight initiative.

8—12	....

. . . 11—15, 20—11; . . . 7—16, 22—18 is less good for Black.

....	28—24
3—8	22—18
16—19	24—15
10—19	23—16
12—19	25—22

White has the initiative.

In this survey of the openings, we have assumed that the games will be started on the "go-as-you-please" principle. This means that the players are free to choose whatever opening sequence they please.

In tournament competitions among experts, it is customary to play under the "three-move restriction" rule. This means that the opening for each game is selected by ballot. The purpose of this is to produce a more spirited type of game and to minimize the emphasis on prepared variations.

Since the average player will never be called upon to start his games in the restricted style, it is not essential for him to study the numerous (more than 130) restricted openings.

While the field of checker openings is extensive and at first sight bewildering, the patterns and standard strategies will become clearer with play; but *plenty of play* is necessary. Only practical experience can drive home the lessons taught by theory. Although theory is a valuable guide, it can never be an adequate substitute for playing experience.

5. How to Win in the Endgame

The inexperienced player is often at a loss to translate material advantage into final victory. Having no clear idea of how to proceed, he drifts in a way that can become very frustrating.

Where you are ahead in material, the guiding principle is *reduction of forces*. In endgames with Kings you bring this about by playing to force your opponent's Kings to the side of the board. In that position, their mobility will be reduced to a minimum, and you can enforce your will.

Two Kings against one is an easy win. Three Kings against two is fairly easy once you have the idea of building a protective bridge, using this as a technique to threaten exchanges.

Four Kings against three is a more difficult proposition, and here you will have your work cut out for you. Such endings make rewarding study because your playing skill will increase accordingly.

Another technique which can often be put to good use in King endings is that of giving up two Kings for one, resolving the position to an ending where you can force a quick win by bottling up the remaining King. Such opportunities occur more frequently than you might imagine.

In all these ways, then, you can force the win systematically and purposefully if you know your goal and are familiar with the techniques that must be used to achieve victory.

Practice these endings until they are second nature. You will frequently encounter these positions, or similar ones, which provide many satisfying opportunities to display your skill.

Diagram 61 (*White to play and win*)

BLACK

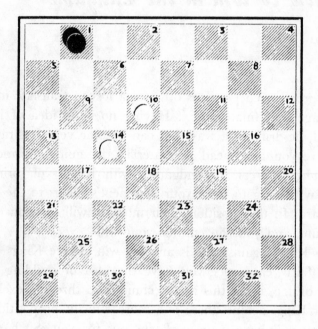

WHITE

The inexperienced player often has trouble winning the endgame of two Kings against one King when the lone King is in the double corner. In the position of Diagram 61, White smokes out the hostile King by forming a protective "bridge."

BLACK	WHITE
....	14—9
1—5	10—14

The bridge is formed.

5—1	9—5
1—6	5—1
6—2	....

Now it would be a waste of time for White to play 14—10, as Black has . . . 2—6 in reply. So:

....	14—18!
2—7	18—15
7—2	15—11

And White wins.

In checkers we have five classic positions which turn up repeatedly in practical play. They are known respectively as First Position, Second Position, Third Position, Fourth Position, and Fifth Position. Because of their practical importance it is well worth studying them until you have thoroughly mastered them.

In First Position (Diagram 62), White has two Kings against one, as in the previous example. But in addition Black has an unmoved man on 3, and this, in the eyes of an inexperienced player, makes the win impossible, or at least exceedingly mysterious.

Actually the win unfolds with enchanting logic and economy of means. Black's object is of course to leave his man on 3 unmoved, for there no harm can befall him.

Hence White first smokes the Black King out of the double corner (as in Diagram 61). The result is that White threatens to trap the Black King on a side square. To avoid this, Black must progressively play . . . 3—8, then . . . 8—12, then . . . 12—16 etc.

Thus the Black man gradually arrives in the orbit of the White Kings, which, by economical play, can simultaneously menace the Black King and the Black man. Superior force must tell, and eventually Black must lose his man; thus White reduces the ending to the situation of Diagram 61 and wins easily.

To the uninitiated player, this may seem a lengthy process, but it is all rigorously worked out and proceeds like clockwork. In studying this ending, it is a good idea to play over the text continuation (columnar moves) first. This will give you a good grasp of the winning method. Once you have accomplished this, you can play over the whole ending again, this time studying the alternative possibilities. Only by examining these alternative possibilities will you arrive at a full appreciation of this beautiful endgame.

Diagram 62 (*White to play and win*)

BLACK

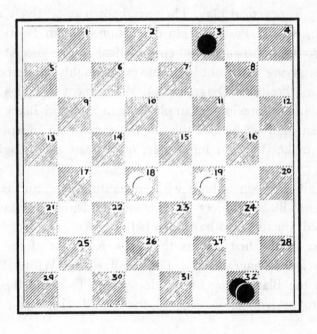

WHITE

BLACK	WHITE
....	18—23
32—28	23—27
28—32	19—23

Again White forms a protective bridge in order to force the Black King out of the double corner. If now . . . 3—7 or . . . 3—8, we simply arrive earlier at the text play.

32—28	27—32

So Black's King must leave the double corner.

28—24	32—28
24—20	23—19!

Forcing Black's reply, for if . . . 3—7 or . . . 3—8, White replies 28—32 and Black's King is bottled up for good.

20—24	19—15
24—27	15—18!

Success! Since . . . 27—32 or . . . 27—31 would now be answered by 18—23 bottling up the Black King, he must move his single man.

3—8	18—15

Forcing Black's next move, for if . . . 27—23, then White replies 28—32, when Black must play . . . 8—12 (since he dare not move his King) leading into the text play after all.

8—12	15—18

Again leaving Black no choice, for if . . . 27—31? White wins with 18—23.

12—16	28—32
27—24	18—15

If Black now plays . . . 16—19 White wins with 32—27!! for after . . . 24—31 White replies 15—24; . . . 31—26, 24—19 (or 24—27) and Black's King will soon be trapped. Here you have a brilliant example of winning simplification.

Diagram 63 (*Black to play, White wins*)

BLACK

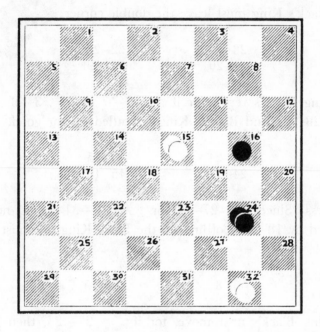

WHITE

Another losing method is for Black now to play . . . 16—20 (from Diagram 63) when there follows 15—18; . . . 24—19, 32—28!; . . . 19—16 (or . . . 20—24, 18—23!!; . . . 19—26, 28—19 and White wins), 18—23; . . . 16—12, 23—19; . . . 12—8 (if . . . 20—24, 19—23 wins), 28—32; . . . 8—11, 32—27; . . . 11—8 (if . . . 11—7, 19—15 wins for White), 27—23. White then continues 23—18 and eventually traps Black's King. Admittedly it requires patience to study these lines of play, but the effort is well worth it.

24—28	15—11!

Forcing another weakening advance. If Black now continues
. . . 16—20, then 11—15; . . . 28—24, 32—28; . . . 24—27,
15—19; . . . 20—24, 19—16 (or 28—32) and White wins.

16—19	32—27
28—32	27—31

If Black tries . . . 19—24 now, White wins after 11—16;
. . . 24—28, 16—20 (or 16—19).

32—28	11—16
19—24	16—19!

But not 16—20?? when Black plays . . . 24—27! or . . . 28—
32! and wins! But after White's last move (forcing . . . 24—27)
he wins the man on 24, remaining with a simple win as shown
in Diagram 61.

Endgames of three Kings against two often baffle the inexperienced player, because he does not know the basic technique
involved. This is to steer relentlessly for an exchange of King
for King, winding up with an easy win of two Kings against one.
Another way is to sacrifice the extra King, leading to a position
which wins because you can trap the remaining King. This is
nicely illustrated in Diagram 64, which at first sight appears
difficult because the weaker side is ensconced in the double
corner.

White's first move looks like a blunder. Actually it is a very
strong move based on a clever finesse.

Diagram 64 (*White to play and win*)

BLACK

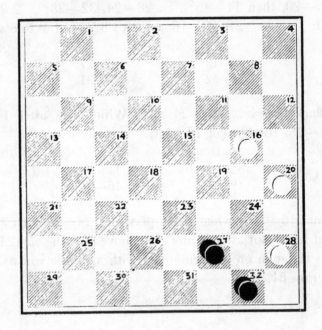

WHITE

BLACK	WHITE
....	16—19!

This looks wrong, for if Black plays . . . 27—24 White must reply 20—27, allowing the two-for-one shot . . . 32—16. But then White continues 28—24 and he must win, as he will quickly force Black's King to a side of the board.

27—31	20—24

If Black now plays . . . 31—26 White replies 19—23! forcing an exchange. Then, after . . . 26—19 White replies 24—15 winning easily. Another case of winning simplification.

32—27	28—32!

A sacrifice that wins at once.

27—20	19—24!
20—27	32—23

And wins, as Black's remaining King is bottled up.

Here is another setting of the three Kings versus two Kings theme which boils down to the same winning technique. However, the situation in Diagram 65 is more difficult in the sense that it takes White some time to arrive at a clearly winning situation.

Diagram 65 (*White to play and win*)

BLACK

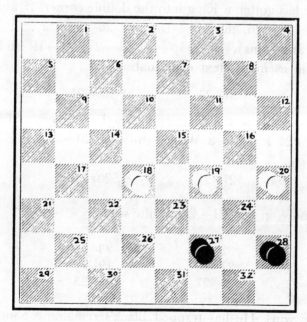

WHITE

White has a plausible try in 19—23, but then Black defends with . . . 28—32. (In that case White does best to return by 23—19, for if instead 23—26??, Black sets up a two-for-one shot with . . . 27—24!, 20—27; . . . 32—14!)

BLACK	WHITE
....	18—15!

White's job is of course to smoke the Black Kings out of the double corner. If Black now plays . . . 27—31, there follows 20—24; . . . 31—26, 15—18; . . . 26—31, 18—23; . . . 28—32, 24—28 and White has taken the first step toward reaching the set-up of Diagram 64.

28—32	19—24
27—31	24—28

White has gotten a King into the double corner. If Black now tries . . . 31—26, then 15—18; . . . 26—31 (or . . . 32—27, 28—32 and wins), 18—23; . . . 31—27, 23—19 and White has a win as in the text continuation.

31—27	15—19!

Now we follow the winning method of Diagram 64. Thus . . . 27—24 leads to a White win after 20—27; . . . 32—16, 28—24 etc.

27—31	20—24

And now on . . . 31—26, White wins by 19—23!

32—27	28—32!
27—20	19—24!
20—27	32—23

White wins. He has trapped Black's remaining King. Again simplification has been the key to the win.

In Diagram 66, White wins by forcing a position in which exchanges are inevitable. To do this, he must build a protective bridge which will prove effective against either Black King.

Diagram 66 (*White to play and win*)

BLACK

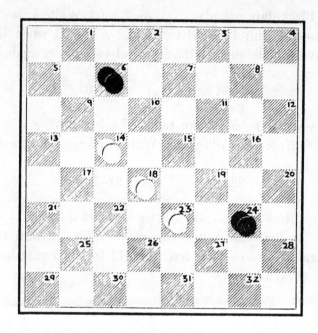

WHITE

White's task seems difficult at first sight, as each Black King has access to a double corner. Nevertheless, White can starve his opponent out of good moves. Again he works by threatening to force exchanges.

BLACK	WHITE
....	18—15!

The necessary preliminary to a later 14—10. If Black now

plays . . . 6—1, we get the text play after 14—10 etc. On the other hand, . . . 6—2?? would be immediately disastrous because of the reply 14—10. Black can prolong his resistance only by hovering around the double corners.

24—28	23—27!

Now Black dare not play . . . 28—32, for White forms a protective bridge with 15—18! forcing . . . 32—23 when 18—27 leaves White with the standard win of two Kings against one.

6—1	14—10!

If now . . . 1—5, White plays 27—24! forcing a winning exchange. Note the skillful use White makes of the protective bridge.

28—32	27—24!

Should Black try . . . 32—28 we now get a beautiful win by 24—19! In that case White answers . . . 28—32 with 10—6!, while against . . . 1—5 he has 19—24! In either case he forces a winning exchange.

1—5	10—6

White is all set to answer . . . 32—28 with 6—10! once more forcing a winning exchange, thanks to his protective bridge.

5—1	24—19!

Once more forming the bridge. Black must play . . . 1—10, and White replies 15—6 with a clear win of two Kings against one. You will find it worth your while to master the technique of winning simplification.

In Diagram 67 (Second Position), material is even. Yet White can win because his position is very superior.

Diagram 67 (*White to play and win*)

BLACK

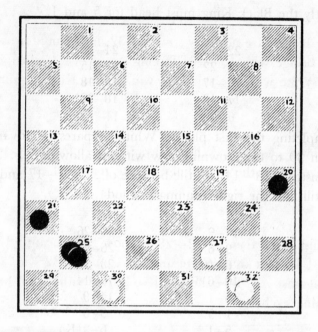

WHITE

Black's men on 20 and 21 are both blocked. White, on the other hand, can arrange matters so that he crowns the men now on 30 and 27. Once he does that, he forces an exchange of Kings and wins very quickly.

Here again the winning process is long but very logical and clear-cut. Study the text play (columnar moves) first, and after you have grasped the winning idea, go back to Diagram 67 and consider the alternative possibilities.

BLACK	WHITE
....	32—28
25—22	28—24

Now Black cannot play . . . 22—25, 24—19; . . . 25—22, 19—23; . . . 22—25?? for then 23—18 wins right off. Consequently the Black King must head for 5 and 1.

22—18	24—19
18—22	19—15
22—17	15—18
17—13	18—22!

Completing the first phase—White prepares to advance his man on 30 to the crowning row without allowing . . . 21—25 etc. (Instead, 18—14 is futile because of . . . 13—17 and White must still find the right winning method).

13—9	30—26
9—6	26—23
6—10	23—18
10—6	18—14
6—1	14—9
1—5	9—6
5—1	6—2(K)

Now White brings his new King to 19, still preventing the Black man on 20 from advancing after White's man on 27 starts for the crowning row.

1—5	2—6
5—1	6—10
1—5	10—15
5—9	15—19
9—14	27—23

At last this advance is feasible.

14—10	23—18
10—6	18—14
6—1	14—9
1—5	9—6
5—1	6—2(K)

Completing another phase. Now White must exchange off Black's King.

Diagram 68 (*Black to play, White wins*)

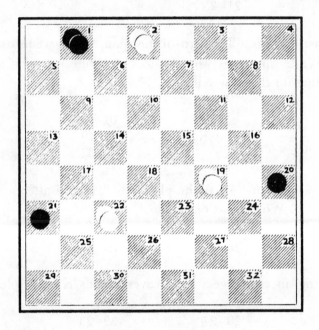

1—5	2—6
5—1	6—10
1—5	10—14
5—1	14—18
1—6	18—23

6—10	23—27
10—14	19—23
14—9	23—18
9—6	18—14
6—1	14—9
1—5	....

The only move Black has left. But now White forces the exchange.

....	22—17!
5—14	17—10
21—25	....

At last Black is able to crown this man, which seems to render all of White's previous work futile. But White will soon succeed in bottling up this new King.

....	10—15
25—30(K)	15—19
30—26	27—32!

If now . . . 26—31 White plays 19—24! and after . . . 20—27, 32—23 White wins on the spot.

26—22	19—24!

Forcing an exchange which leaves Black's King helpless.

20—27	32—23

And White wins in two more moves.

Diagram 69 shows another setting for an endgame of three Kings versus two. Again the problem is one of forcing the weaker side out of the double corner. Again the winning side makes use of the simplifying technique, which involves: (a) exchanging King for King, leading into a winning endgame of two Kings against one; or (b) sacrificing two Kings for one, in order to force a position that is even in material but won for White because he can trap the remaining Black King.

Diagram 69 (*White to play and win*)

BLACK

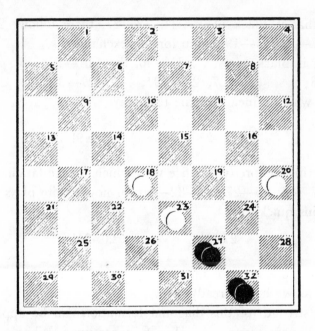

WHITE

White aims to transfer his King from 23 to 24 in order to drive Black's King from 27 to 31, where the latter can be bottled up.

BLACK	WHITE
....	23—19
32—28	18—15

Now Black has no choice, for if . . . 27—32?? then 19—23 wins immediately for White.

28—32	19—24

Forcing Black's reply, since after . . . 27—23 White can bring about an immediate exchange with 15—19.

27—31	24—28

So that if Black plays . . . 32—27, there follows 28—32; . . . 27—23, 15—19, again forcing exchanges.

And if Black tries . . . 31—26, then 15—18; . . . 26—31, 18—23; . . . 31—27, 23—19!; . . . 27—31, 20—24! and White wins by means of the text play.

31—27	15—19!

Offering the pretty sacrifice with which we are familiar, thus: . . . 27—24, 20—27; . . . 32—16 for now White plays 28—24 and wins quickly.

27—31	20—24!

Once more constructing a bridge—a valuable winning technique, as we have already seen.

The strength of this diagonal formation can be appreciated if Black now plays . . . 31—26, whereupon White's 19—23 forces a winning simplifying exchange.

32—27	....

Now one would think that White has nothing better than the humdrum 24—20, stamping his last move as a wasted move. Instead, White has the familiar winning sacrifice.

....	28—32!
27—20	19—24!
20—27	32—23

And White has won the game.

One of the most difficult endings to win is two Kings plus a single man against two Kings. In fact, there are many drawing situations arising such as Payne's Draw (Diagram 91) and Roger's Draw (Diagram 93).

A standard winning position of this type appears in Third Position (Diagram 70).

Diagram 70 (*Black to play and win*)

BLACK

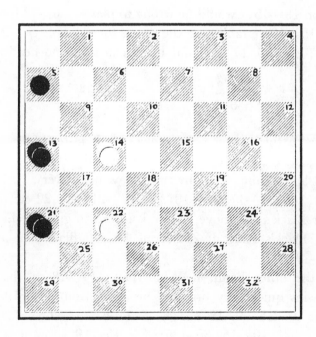

WHITE

Black's problem is to advance his single man to the King row, or, in the event that White maintains the blockade, to find some compensating advantage.

Once more, since the winning process is a lengthy one, it is advisable to go over the main play first and consider the alternatives later.

BLACK	WHITE
13—9	22—18

Here 14—10? or 14—18? would be a blunder because of . . . 9—14, forcing an exchange that wins easily for White.

9—6	....

If White now tries 18—15, Black's best course is . . . 6—2! leading into the text line.

But on 18—15 it would be wrong to play . . . 6—1? for White replies 15—10! establishing the draw, for example . . . 21—25, 14—17; 25—30, 17—14 and Black can make no headway.

....	18—22
6—1!	....

But *now* this is the right move, for if instead . . . 6—2?, 14—10; . . . 5—9, 10—6; . . . 9—13, 6—10; . . . 21—17, 22—18 and White draws by the seesaw maneuver . . . 17—21, 18—22; . . . 21—17, 22—18; . . . 17—21, 18—22 etc.

After Black's last move, White is forced to give up the blockade on Black's King at 21; for if 14—10 Black can advance . . . 5—9.

On the other hand, if White plays 14—18 at this stage, Black wins quickly by bringing his King from 1 to 19 in this fashion: . . . 5—9, 18—23; . . . 1—6, 23—26; . . . 6—10, 26—30; . . . 10—15, 30—26; . . . 15—19 (now it is only a matter of time until Black lifts the blockade on his King at 21),

26—30; . . 19—23, 22—26; . . . 23—18 (the blockade is
lifted!), 26—31; . . . 18—22, 31—27 (if 30—26 Black wins
easily with . . . 9—13); . . . 21—17, 27—31; . . . 9—14 and
Black soon gets a new King with an easy win.

Diagram 71 (*White to play, Black wins*)

BLACK

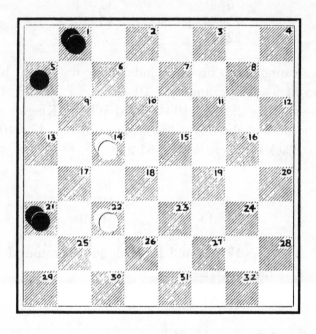

WHITE

| .... | 22—18 |
| 21—25 | .... |

Black immediately pops out of the blockade.

Should White try 14—17, he allows the man on 5 to advance,
for example . . . 5—9, 17—21; . . . 9—14! (beautiful), 18—9;
. . . 1—5 (the point!), 21—30; . . . 5—14 and Black wins

quickly by bottling up the White King. Thus if 30—26; . . . 14—18 etc.

Another possibility after 14—17; . . . 5—9 is 18—15; . . . 25—21, 17—22; . . . 21—17! with a fireworks finish, as after 22—6 Black makes a clean sweep with . . . 1—19.

....	18—15
1—6!	14—17
6—2!	17—14
25—22	15—10
22—26	....

White cannot keep his King indefinitely on 14 (to blockade the man at 5). For example, if 10—15; . . . 26—23, 15—18; . . . 23—19, 18—22; . . . 19—15 and White's King at 14 must depart because of the threat to exchange by . . . 15—10. (This explains Black's earlier . . . 1—6! and . . . 6—2!)

....	14—18
5—9	10—6
9—13	6—10

Now . . . 13—17?? would be a blunder because of White's "breeches" stratagem 18—22!

26—31!	....

This threatens . . . 13—17.

....	10—14

Forced, to stop . . . 13—17. But now Black's King is freed from his imprisonment at 2.

31—27	....

This King has to swing around to cooperate with the other Black King.

....	18—22
27—23	....

Contemplating this possibility: 14—10; . . . 23—19, 10—14; . . . 19—15, 14—9; . . . 15—10 and Black has reached the final text winning set-up.

....	22—25
2—7	....

At this point Black must be constantly on his guard against Payne's Draw (Diagram 91).

....	25—22
7—11	....

Diagram 72 (*White to play, Black wins*)

BLACK

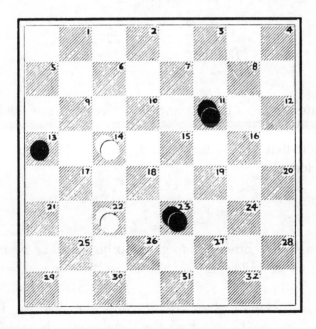

WHITE

If White now plays 22—18 we get . . . 23—27, 18—22; . . . 11—15, 22—26 (not 14—18? because of . . . 13—17! and wins); . . . 27—24, 26—22; . . . 24—20, 22—26; . . . 20—16, 26—22; . . . 16—12 and Black wins by playing . . . 12—8 followed by . . . 8—3. This forces the King on 14 to move because of the threat of . . . 15—10.

....	22—25
11—15	25—22
23—27	22—26
27—24	26—22
24—20	22—26
20—16	26—22
16—12	....

This King is heading toward 3. Black is following the procedure outlined in the previous note.

....	22—26
12—8	26—22
8—3	....

Threatening . . . 15—10 and thus forcing White's King on 14 to move.

But note that 14—17 is refuted by . . . 15—18! Thus White's reply is forced.

....	14—9
15—10	....

This wins, for either White gives up his blockade by moving his King on 22 (allowing . . . 13—17 etc.) or we get 9—5; . . . 10—14, 5—1; . . . 3—7, 1—5; . . . 7—10, 5—1; . . . 10—15!, 1—5; . . . 14—18, 22—25; and now the man on 13 can advance . . . 13—17, reaching the King row fairly rapidly and giving Black three Kings to two for a win.

A situation with four Kings against three Kings often puzzles inexperienced players. The solution (as in Diagram 73) lies in forcing an exchange of Kings, thus reducing to the manageable ending of three Kings against two.

Diagram 73 (*White to play and win*)

WHITE

With his first move, White completes the bottling-up process for the Black Kings on 30 and 31. However, the remaining Black King in the double corner remains free. This creates a problem for White, but he can solve it.

BLACK	WHITE
....	20—24

Leaving Black with only one move.

32—28	23—19

If Black now plays . . . 30—26, then 24—20 forcing an exchange that leaves White with three Kings against two.

28—32	24—28

Cutting down Black's activities in the double corner. If now . . . 32—27, 28—32 forces a winning exchange for White.

31—27	19—16

Setting up another opportunity for a winning exchange, thus: . . . 27—23, 28—24; . . . 32—28, 24—19; . . . 23—27, 22—26 etc.

27—31	16—20

This leaves Black with little choice, for if . . . 32—27, 28—32; . . . 27—23, 20—24; and now, after . . . 30—26 or . . . 23—26, Black is forced into a simplifying exchange that wins easily for White.

31—27	22—26!!

This leads to a neat two-for-one win, or, in any event, a winning exchange.

30—23	28—24

Now Black could prolong the agony—though in a losing fight—by forgetting about the loss of his King on 27 and playing . . . 23—18. Instead, Black tries to save the vulnerable King—and loses to a different simplifying maneuver.

27—31	24—27!
31—24	20—18

And White wins easily with two Kings against one.

In Diagram 74 we have a similar position, which in fact winds up with the same winning process.

Diagram 74 (*White to play and win*)

BLACK

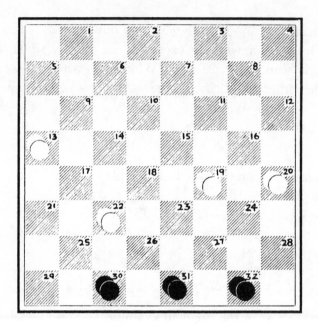

WHITE

Here too Black's resistance is based on his occupation of the double corner.

BLACK	WHITE
....	19—24

Note that if Black now plays . . . 30—26, he simply hastens his defeat, as White replies with a meaningless waiting move, keeping his Kings on 22 and 13 at their respective squares. Then

Black must exchange, and White has an easy win with three Kings against two.

And if Black plays . . . 32—28, White simply plays 24—27 similarly forcing a winning exchange.

32—27	24—28
27—32	....

If instead . . . 27—23, 28—32 and now . . . 23—26 or . . . 30—26 leads to a winning exchange for White, while if . . . 23—19 (instead of : . . 23—26) White wins with 32—27.

On the other hand, if . . . 27—23, 28—32; . . . 31—27, 22—26! wins for White.

....	13—17!

A valuable waiting move. If Black plays . . . 30—26, White simply replies 17—13! (or 17—21!) and wins.

If Black tries . . . 32—27, 28—32; . . . 27—23, then 20—24 wins. For on . . . 23—26 or . . . 30—26 White still wins with 17—13 (or 17—21).

31—27	22—26!!

White wins as in the previous example.

30—23	28—24

And White wins, as . . . 27—31 allows a two-for-one shot by 24—27; . . . 31—24, 20—18; and . . . 23—18 allows White to play 24—31 with three Kings against two.

Similar, and yet in some ways different, is the situation we find in Fourth Position (Diagram 75). The play is so delicate that Black can win only if it is his turn to move. If White moves first (see the play following Diagram 89) the game is a draw!

Here again, since the weaker side has many alternative possibilities, it is advisable to play over the main line first before examining the alternative moves.

Diagram 75 (*Black to play and win*)

BLACK

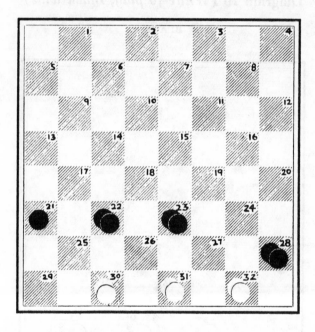

WHITE

Black has several possible methods of winning. One is to force an exchange of Kings. Another is to entice the advance of White's King on 30, in order to facilitate the advance of Black's man on 21 to the King row. Still another method, which turns up in several variations, is a neat sacrifice which forces either an exchange of Kings or a two-for-one win (in a situation which reminds us of the win based on Diagram 74).

BLACK	WHITE
28—24	32—28
24—20	28—32
22—18	....

Black's "retreat" is purely a matter of strategy. He is rearranging his forces for more effective operations.

Diagram 76 (*White to play, Black wins*)

BLACK

WHITE

Right now White must watch his step, for if 32—28 Black forces a winning exchange with . . . 23—27.

On 31—26, however, the win is more involved. There follows . . . 23—19, 32—27; . . . 19—24, 27—32 (if 27—31?; . . . 20—16 wins); . . . 24—28, 26—31 (if 32—27; . . . 28—32

wins); .. 18—23, 31—27 (if 31—26; . . . 20—24 wins);
. . . 23—26!, 30—23; . . . 28—24 and Black wins (27—31;
. . . 24—27!), as we have seen in a previous position. (This
motif turns up repeatedly in the following play.)

Again, if 31—26 (this is still from Diagram 76); . . . 23—19,
32—27; . . . 19—24, 26—31; . . . 24—28, 31—26 (if 27—32;
. . . 18—23 wins as in the previous variation); . . . 28—32 wins
as above.

		31—27
	23—19	

If now 32—28; . . . 18—22, 28—32; . . . 19—24 (intending
to answer 27—23 with . . . 24—19 forcing a winning exchange),
27—31; . . . 24—28 (so that if 31—27 Black wins with . . .
22—26!, 30—23; . . . 28—24), 32—27; . . . 28—32, 27—23;
. . . 20—24, 30—26; . . . 24—27! again forcing a winning
exchange.

		27—31
	19—24	

(See Diagram 77)

And now again on 32—28 Black wins with . . . 24—27
forcing an exchange.

More involved is 31—26; . . . 24—28 with these possibilities:

(I) 32—27; . . . 28—32, 26—23; . . . 18—22, 27—31;
. . . 20—24, 30—26 (if 23—26?? Black wins at once with . . .
22—18), . . . 24—27! forcing an exchange that wins for Black.

(II) 26—31; . . . 18—23. Then if 31—27; . . . 23—26!,
30—23; . . . 28—24 wins; or if 31—26; . . . 20—24 forces a
winning exchange for Black.

Diagram 77 (*White to play, Black wins*)

BLACK

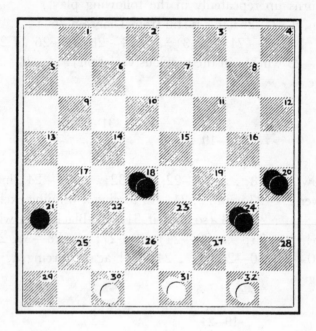

WHITE

....	32—27
24—28	....

The beginning of the end, for on 31—26 there follows . . .
28—32, 26—23; . . . 18—22 winning as in Variation I above.

....	27—32
18—23!	....

Setting the stage for the final coup. If now 31—26; . . . 20—
24 forces a winning exchange.

```
                              31—27
        23—26!                ........
```

The long-prepared sacrifice.

```
        ........                30—23
        28—24                  ........
```

And Black wins the King on 27, for if 27—31; . . . 24—27,
31—24; . . . 20—18 etc. In either case Black will crown his
remaining man and then win the standard ending of three Kings
against two, or two Kings against one.

The great lesson to be learned from these endings is that with
three Kings against two, or four Kings against three, your aim
should be to exchange relentlessly.

A subsidiary technique which you can often apply is to sacrifice two Kings for one, winding up in an endgame which is
even in material but which you win because you can trap the
remaining hostile King.

Remember that when you are ahead in material, you must
force your opponent's Kings to the side. There they will have
the least mobility, enabling you to enforce your threats with the
minimum of resistance to your plans.

6. How to Draw "Lost" Positions

While the beginner is eager to win and considers winning a laudable ambition, he often lacks the proper attitude toward the draw. There are many desperate situations in checker games where it is quite a feat to be able to draw what is to all appearances a lost game. It is a good player's particular delight to salvage such positions from disaster.

A common drawing motif is based on the idea of taking advantage of an unfavorable corner or side situation of the numerically stronger side. (As we know, checker forces have little mobility at the side and even less in the single corner.) By skillful and economical use of your forces you can often work wonders to achieve a draw even though outnumbered.

Sometimes a nicely prepared two-for-one shot will do the trick, restoring material equality. In other cases, perfect timing of temporary sacrifices is the answer. A position may be lost if you play the orthodox, "safe" way. Yet if you transpose moves—change their order—you may produce a finesse that just saves the game. Or, by means of a clever "seesaw" maneuver you may be able to hold your opponent at bay despite his material superiority. Quick, careless moves or acceptance of the inevitable are sure to lose; whereas deft, resourceful, foresighted play will make all the difference.

There are also a number of exceedingly valuable endgame positions which can be drawn when you are down in material.

You should practice the correct moves until you know them by heart and can apply them in your own games.

In general, these drawing positions are based on the following principle: the outnumbered forces are placed very favorably and can operate at maximum effectiveness. The numerically stronger forces, on the other hand, are split and cannot do their best. The extra single man, for example, is generally at the side and cannot advance. Watch this principle in operation and you will save many a "lost" game.

When you are down in material, you can often force a draw if your opponent's men are in and near a single corner. As we see in Diagram 78, the numerically stronger side has very little mobility in such situations.

Diagram 78 (*White to play and draw*)

BLACK

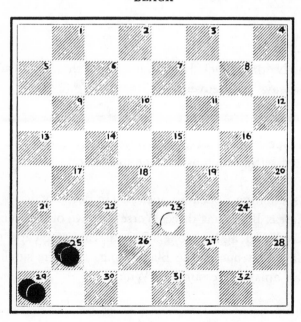

WHITE

White's King is perfectly poised for the draw. (Note, however, that if it were Black's move, he could break out of the unfavorable formation with . . . 25—22, winning easily as in Diagram 61.)

BLACK	WHITE
....	23—26!

Of course 23—18?? would be a terrible blunder, allowing Black to win offhand with . . . 25—22.

| 25—21 | 26—22 |

This is the move that holds the draw.

| 21—25 | 22—26 |

Or 22—17 with the same effect.

| 25—30 | 26—22 |

Drawn. Neither Black King can escape, thanks to the White King's "seesaw" maneuver.

This theme is very useful to know, as we can see in a more complicated setting such as the one in Diagram 79.

White's situation appears hopeless. He does not have a single King, whereas Black has three. Worse yet, two of the White men are attacked and at least one of them cannot escape capture. Yet the fact that one of the Black Kings is in the single corner suggests an amazing resource to White.

Diagram 79 (*White to play and draw*)

BLACK

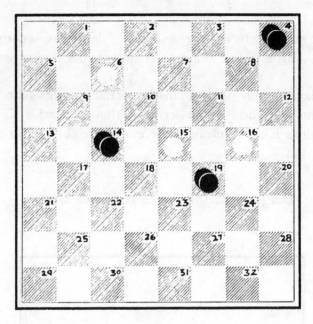

WHITE

BLACK	WHITE
....	15—10!

Since White must lose a man anyway, he loses it in the most advantageous way.

If now . . . 14—7, 6—2(K); . . . 19—12, 2—11 and lo and behold! White has the drawing position of Diagram 78. An exquisite line of play.

19—12	6—2(K)

This transposes into the previous note!

$$14-7 \qquad\qquad 2-11$$

And again White has the desperately desired seesaw drawing position. This is a fine example of split-second timing.

In Diagram 80 White is in dire straits, as his man on 29 cannot move. Worse yet, it seems as though Black's King can trap White's King. We might therefore carelessly conclude that White is lost.

Diagram 80 (*White to play and draw*)

BLACK

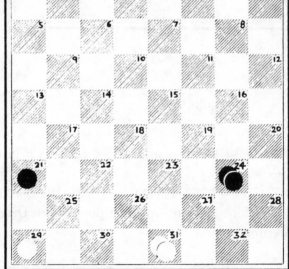

WHITE

Despite the desperate character of this position, White can draw if he forces the Black King to the side.

BLACK	WHITE
....	31—26
24—19	26—30

Of course not 26—31?? when . . . 19—23 wins for Black at once.

19—23	29—25
23—18	....

Now it seems to be all over, as White must lose a man. Yet the draw is there!

....	25—22!
18—25	30—26
25—29	....

If . . . 25—30, 26—22 and the man on 21 must move, establishing the draw at once.

....	26—30

Also possible, but more complicated, is 26—22; . . . 21—25, 22—26; . . . 25—30(K), 26—22 and White draws as in Diagram 78.

29—25	30—26

And White draws by the seesaw maneuver, as Black cannot escape from the pattern.

Another, very similar example turns up in Diagram 81. Here White is apparently lost, as Black gets a two-for-one shot after 9—14??; . . . 23—26, 30—23; . . . 27—9—or else 25—22??; . . . 23—26, 30—23; . . . 27—25.

Diagram 81 (*White to play and draw*)

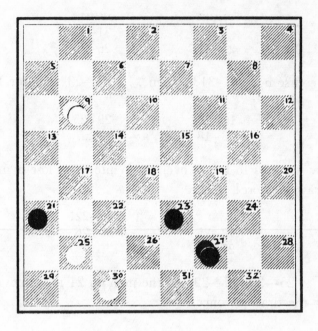

WHITE

Nevertheless White can draw if he plays for the seesaw pattern.

BLACK	WHITE
....	9—13!

The only way to draw.

23—26	30—23
27—18	....

Now White must lose his man on 25, which is equivalent to the loss of the game—or is it?

Forced, but good just the same.

| 18—25 | 13—17 |
| 25—29 | .... |

If . . . 25—30, 17—22 and White draws at once.

| .... | 17—22 |
| 21—25 | 22—26 |

Now Black gets a second King . . . but still cannot win, as we saw in a note to the previous example.

| 25—30(K) | 26—22 |
| 30—25 | 22—26 |

Also feasible is 22—17—but not 22—18??; . . . 25—22 and wins.

25—21	26—22
21—25	22—26
25—30	26—22

And White draws by the seesaw maneuver.

Even when there is no question of the single corner involved, the numerically weaker side has valuable resources if the other player's forces are confined to the side of the board. In Diagram 82 White would be lost if it were Black's move, for then the man on 11 would rush on to the King row. But with White to move first, he forces an easy draw.

Diagram 82 (*White to play and draw*)

BLACK

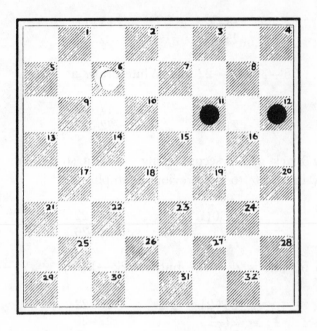

WHITE

White hastens to prevent . . . 11—15.

BLACK	WHITE
....	6—10!

If now . . . 12—16, 10—7; . . . 11—15, 7—11 drawing.

BLACK	WHITE
11—16	10—15
16—20	15—19
12—16	....

Forced.

BLACK	WHITE
....	19—12
20—24	....

Drawn.

And in Diagram 83 White is able to hold the hostile forces at bay, again because it is his move. (If Black moves first, he wins easily.)

Diagram 83 (*White to play and draw*)

BLACK

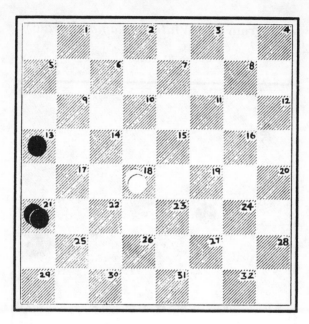

WHITE

White finds the right move to tie up Black's forces:

BLACK	WHITE
....	18—22
21—17	22—18

Leaving Black no choice.

17—21	18—22

Drawn. Black has no way out of the seesaw pattern.

Now let us see how the pattern can be applied in a more elaborate setting. There are many positions where the most obvious order of moves will lose; on the other hand, if you modify the order slightly, you can transform the loss into a draw. Diagram 84 offers a fine example of this. (Compare this situation with Diagram 30.)

Diagram 84 (*White to play and draw*)

BLACK

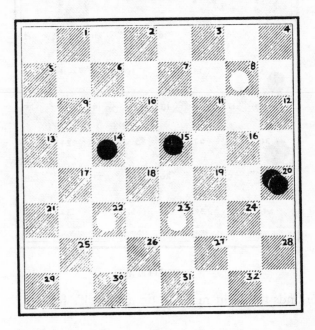

WHITE

Well may White wring his hands in despair. If he plays the most natural move, 8—3(K)?? or 8—4(K)??, there follows . . . 15—19!, 23—16; . . . 20—11, and, having starved White out of moves, Black wins on the spot.

And, since White cannot move his men on 22 and 23, he is seemingly lost.

But there is a way out:

BLACK   WHITE
....   23—19!

So this man can move after all! Here is White's reasoning. By means of this sacrifice, he will evade the ruinous line shown in the previous note. Then, once he gets a King, he will go after Black's man on 14, and thus reestablish material equality with a drawn position.

15—24	8—3(K)
24—27	3—7
27—31(K)	7—10
31—26	10—17

Drawn—and just in the nick of time. A splendid ending.

By way of review, let us return to the seesaw theme. Without this finesse, White would be hopelessly lost in the position of Diagram 85.

Diagram 85 (*White to play and draw*)

BLACK

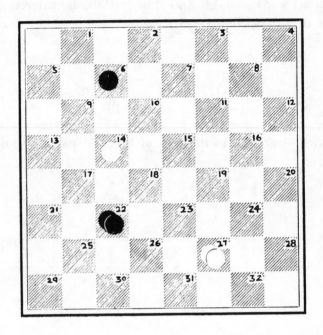

WHITE

Black threatens to gobble up the man on 14 by playing . . . 22—18 or . . . 22—17. It would seem at first sight that White's King is too far off to lend a hand, but actually he is a very acrobatic King who can work miracles.

BLACK	WHITE
....	27—23!

The beauty of this move is that it looks like a horrible blunder allowing the "breeches" trick . . . 22—18. But in that case White draws with the sly move 14—9! or 14—10!

22—17   ....

This is the only move worth considering, and of course Black still expects to win; but dwell for a moment on the alternative . . . 22—25?? This is a fearsome blunder which allows White to seize the initiative at once with 23—18 or 23—26 winning.

....   14—9!

White relies on the old faithful seesaw pattern. (See Diagram 83.)

6—13	23—18
17—21	18—22
21—17	22—18
17—21	18—22

Drawn. Black can make no headway while White holds the fort with his seesaw maneuver.

White is in a bad way in Diagram 86. He wants to crown another King to even up matters, but after 6—2(K) Black wins the man on 11 with . . . 10—7; and on 6—1(K) instead, Black still wins with . . . 19—16.

Diagram 86 (*White to play and draw*)

BLACK

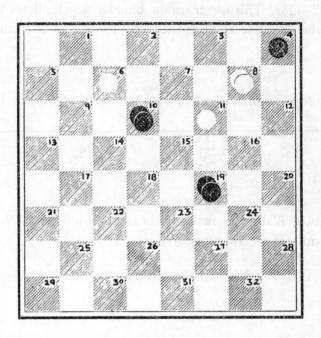

WHITE

White can draw, despite appearances, by two very pretty sacrifices perfectly timed.

BLACK	WHITE
....	6–2(K)!

The only way to save the game.

10—7 ....

Apparently decisive, as the man on 11 is lost. The question is: What is the best way to lose it?

....   8—12!

A brilliant finesse.

7—16   ....

It is still not apparent that White has gained. But note that Black's numerically superior forces have only one reply left after White's next move.

....   2—7
16—20   ....

Forced; but now White's bombshell bursts.

....   12—8!

Laying the groundwork for a neat two-for-one shot that re-establishes material equality.

4—11   7—23

Drawn. Very pretty play.

Now back again to our old friend the seesaw theme. In Diagram 87 Black is on the point of losing material, as his men on 22 and 23 are both attacked. On . . . 23—26? White replies 18—25 and wins.

Diagram 87 (*Black to play and draw*)

BLACK

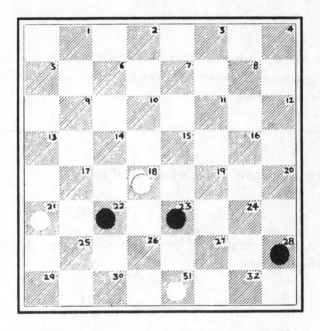

WHITE

If Black plays . . . 28—32(K) White of course does not capture 18—27? Instead he plays 18—25 and wins. But by a little trick Black can turn the whole transaction to his advantage.

BLACK	WHITE
22—26!	....

Looks nonsensical, but there is method in his madness.

If now 18—27 Black replies . . . 28—32(K)!, 31—22; . . .
32—23 drawing as in the text continuation.

	31—22
28—32(K)!	....

The point of Black's sacrifice.

	18—27
32—23	....

Now we have reduced the position to the same situation as
in Diagram 82 (with colors reversed), in which the draw is
forced.

Thus if now 21—17; . . . 23—26, 22—18; . . . 26—22 and
Black draws at once.

	22—17
23—18	17—13
18—14	21—17

Forced; but now Black replies . . . 14—21 and the game is
drawn.

Before we turn to some standard drawing positions, here is a beautiful example of profound and resourceful play. In Diagram 88 Black is a man down, and is naturally eager to recover it. However, he sees that the obvious . . . 27—23? will not do.

Diagram 88 (*Black to play and draw*)

BLACK

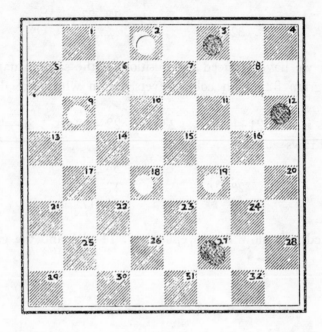

WHITE

The reason that . . . 27—23? will not do is this: the play goes 18—15!; . . . 23—16, 15—11!; . . . 16—7, 2—11 and White wins.

Yet there *is* a way for Black to draw:

BLACK	WHITE
3—7!!	....

An amazing resource.

Now this move works for Black.

The point is that Black threatens *two* two-for-one shots:
. . . 23—7 or . . . 23—5. White must allow one or the other,
after which the game is drawn. This is a real object lesson in
perfect timing.

Now let us turn to some of the standard endgame drawing
positions. In the case of Fourth Position (Diagram 75) we saw
that the stronger side can win *if it is his turn to move*. But the
weaker side can draw if it is his move. We repeat the position
in Diagram 89.

Diagram 89 (*White to play and draw*)

BLACK

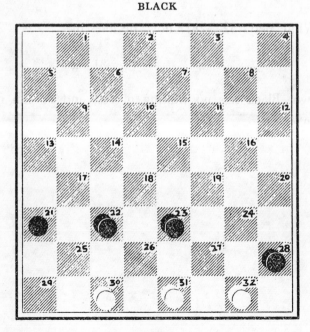

WHITE

Not having the move, Black can never smoke his opponent out of the double corner, and he can never force the two-for-one shot characteristic of the play from Diagram 75.

BLACK	WHITE
....	31—27
23—19	27—31
19—24	32—27

Black has no time to occupy the double corner.

24—20	27—32

White dashes right back into the double corner.

22—18	31—27
28—24	27—31
18—23	....

If White plays 32—28?? now, he loses by . . . 24—27.

....	31—26

Drawn. Black has no waiting moves, and he can make no headway.

Fifth Position, illustrated in Diagram 90, turns up often enough to be worth knowing. It has saved many an apparently lost game.

Diagram 90 (*White to play and draw*)

BLACK

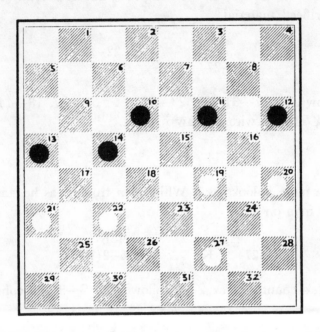

WHITE

(This position can also arise with colors reversed.)

The set-up looks alarming for White, as he must lose material no matter what he plays. On the plausible-looking 27—23?, for instance, Black has . . . 11—15 in reply.

BLACK	WHITE
....	20—16!

This sacrifice, getting rid of Black's troublesome man on 11, is the key to the following play.

11—20	27—23
20—24	....

Black is on the way to the King row, but now White regains the sacrificed material.

....	22—18
24—27	18—9

If now . . . 27—31(K), 23—18; . . . 31—27, 18—14; . . . 10—17, 21—14 with a draw in sight.

10—14	....

Once more it looks as if White is in trouble, as he stands to lose his man on 23.

....	9—6
27—31(K)	6—2(K)

White's counterattack 2—6 followed by 6—9 will come just in time.

31—27	2—6!
27—18	6—9
13—17	19—15!

Breaks up Black's formation to get a two-for-one transaction.

18—11	9—18

Drawn. Black cannot save the man at 17.

Another famous position, Payne's Draw, is really an adaptation of the seesaw technique which we have seen so many times, for example in Diagram 78.

Diagram 91 (*White to play and draw*)

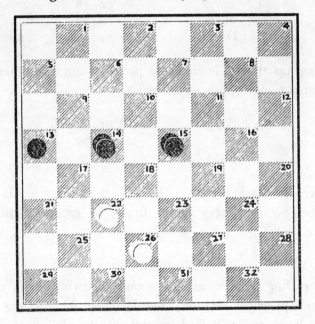

WHITE

White takes advantage of the fact that the man on 13 can never advance, nor can the Black Kings dislodge the White Kings from their favorable position.

BLACK	WHITE
....	26—23!

This keeps the stone wall intact.

14—17	23—26
15—10	....

On . . . 15—11 the same reply serves.

....	22—18
10—6	26—30
17—21	....

Taking up the futile side-row position, but the other Black King cannot accomplish anything.

....	18—22
6—9	30—26
9—14	26—30

Drawn. If Black tries . . . 14—17??, he loses a King after 22—18. This is a very useful draw, of great practical importance.

The ending known as Petterson's Drawbridge is another useful and practical position (See Diagram 92.) As the ending is fairly long, you will find it advisable to play over the text continuation first, and then examine the alternative lines of play later on.

White's choice of moves is limited, and he must use his resources with great delicacy.

Thus, if 20—16?; . . . 23—19, 16—12; . . . 19—15, 2—6; . . . 15—11, 6—9 (or 6—2; . . . 22—18, 21—17; . . . 18—14 and Black wins); . . . 11—7, 9—14; . . . 22—17 Black wins.

So White must choose a different way.

Diagram 92 (*White to play and draw*)

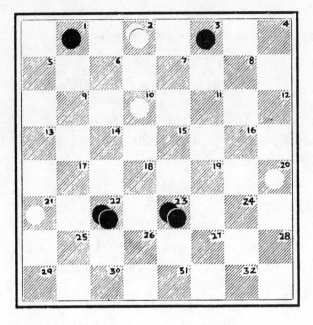

WHITE

BLACK	WHITE
	2—7
23—19	7—2

Now it will not do for Black to play . . . 19—15? as White has the spare move 20—16.

22—18	2—7

And now Black's mistake . . . 18—14? is refuted by 7—2; while . . . 3—8?? allows 10—6!; . . . 1—10, 7—16 and White wins!

The further advance of this man will be used to force an exchange which Black hopes will win for him.

	7—2
....	
19—15	2—6!

White avoids 10—6?; . . . 5—9, 6—1(K); . . . 3—7 and Black wins! 2—11; . . . 15—8, 20—16; . . . 18—14! followed by . . . 9—13 and . . . 13—17 etc.

| 5—9 | 6—13 |
| 15—6 | .... |

Now White can still go wrong with 21—17? . . . 3—7, 20—16; . . . 7—10, 16—12; . . . 18—14 and Black wins.

| .... | 20—16! |
| 18—22 | 21—17! |

And here White can still escape, if Black tries . . . 22—18, 16—12; . . . 3—7, 12—8; . . . 7—10, 8—3(K)!; . . . 18—14, 3—7!

| 6—10 | 16—12 |

Now both sides get new Kings, leading to an exciting finish. An exquisite point here is that Black dare not move his King from 22, for then 17—14!! wins for White!

| 3—7 | 12—8 |
| 7—11 | 8—3(K) |

White must find a defense to Black's plan of getting a new King at 30 and then playing . . . 30—25 followed by . . . 25—21.

11—15	3—8
15—18	8—11!
18—23	11—16
23—26	16—19
26—30(K)	19—23
30—25	....

All set to play . . . 25—21. But White has a wonderful
resource.

....	17—14!
10—17	23—18!
22—15	13—29

Winding up a beautiful compound stroke for a draw.

We conclude this chapter with Roger's Draw, another standard drawing position. In Diagram 93 we note that White, although a man down, has a comparatively good situation for his pieces.

Diagram 93 (*White to play and draw*)

BLACK

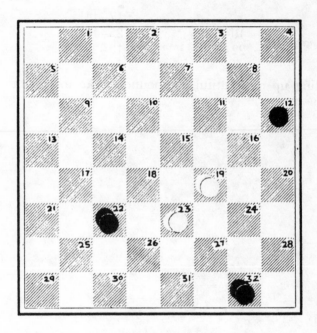

WHITE

The first thing that catches the eye in Diagram 93 is that Black's forces are split. They do not cooperate and cannot be made to do so. The extra man on 12 is of very little use, as it can always be captured if it advances. Nor can Black's King at 32 escape from the double corner with any useful effect.

After a few futile efforts, Black will come to realize that he cannot make any headway.

BLACK	WHITE
....	19—24

Of course . . . 12—16 would be pointless in reply, as White simply plays 24—20.

22—17	24—19
17—14	19—24
14—10	23—19
32—28	24—20

Obviously Black's prospects have not improved.

10—7	19—15
28—32	20—24

He does not allow . . . 32—27.

7—2	24—19

Drawn. Black can never make any useful headway toward advancing his man from 12.

In these examples you have seen repeatedly how economical deployment of your outnumbered forces can save the day. Throughout this chapter you have seen many instances of practical resources you can use in your own games. Above all, be on the lookout to avoid unfavorable exchanges which may cripple your chances of resistance.

APPENDIX I

The Standard Laws of Checkers

1. The Standard Board

The Standard Board must be of 64 light and dark squares. The board must be placed so that each player has a dark single corner at his left hand.

2. The Standard Men

The Standard Men, technically described as Black and White, must be light and dark (e.g., white and red, or white and black), and round.

3. Placement of the Men

The men shall be placed on the dark squares.

The Black men shall invariably be placed upon the first dark twelve squares of the board (numbered 1 to 12) the White men upon the last twelve dark squares (numbered 21 to 32).

4. Order of Playing

Each player shall play alternate games with Black and White men, and lots shall be cast for the color only once—at the commencement of a match, the winner to have the choice of taking either Black or White.

The first move must invariably be made by the player having the Black men.

5. *Time Limit for Playing*

At the end of five minutes (if the move has not been previously made), "Time" must be called distinctly by the person appointed for the purpose; if the move be not completed at the expiration of another minute, the game shall be adjudged as lost through improper delay.

When there is only one way of taking one or more men, "Time" shall be called at the end of one minute; if the move be not completed at the expiration of another minute, the game shall be adjudged as lost through improper delay.

6. *Arrangement of the Men during a Game*

Either player is entitled, on giving intimation, to arrange his own or his opponent's men properly on the squares. After the first move has been made, however, if either player touches any man without giving intimation, he shall be cautioned for the first offense, and shall forfeit the game for any subsequent act of the kind.

7. *Touch and Move*

After the men have been arranged, if the player whose turn it is to play, touches one, he must either move that man or forfeit the game. When the piece is not playable, he is penalized according to the preceding law.

If any part of a playable man is moved over an angle of the square on which it is stationed, the play must be completed in that direction.

8. Capturing Play

A capturing play, as well as an ordinary one, is completed whenever the hand is withdrawn from the piece played, even though more than one man has been taken. The play whereby a single man captures an opposing man or men into the opposing crown row constitutes a move and the capturing man becomes a King. It is then the opposing side's turn to play.

9. Removal of Men

When capturing, if a player removes one of his own men, he cannot replace it, but his opponent can either play or insist on his replacing it.

10. False or Improper Move

If either player makes a false or improper move, he shall instantly forfeit the game to his opponent.

11. Crowning of Men

When a man reaches, for the first time, any of the squares on the opposite extreme line of the board, technically called the "King Row," it becomes a "King" and can be moved backward or forward as the limits of the board permit (though not in the same play—see Rule 8) and must be "crowned" (by placing a man on top of it) by the opponent; but, if said opponent neglects to do so and plays, such play shall be put back until the man is crowned.

12. Drawn Games

A "draw" comes about when neither player can force a win. (A win results when one player captures or blocks all of his opponent's pieces, or when any violation of the preceding or subsequent laws takes place.) When one side appears stronger than the other, the player of the stronger side is required to complete the win, or to show (to the satisfaction of the Umpire or Referee) at least a decided advantage over his opponent within forty of his own moves—said moves to be counted from the point at which notice was given, failing in which he must relinquish the game as a draw.

13. Conduct of Players and Spectators

Anything which may tend to annoy or distract the attention of the players is strictly forbidden—such as making signs or sounds, pointing or hovering over the board, or unnecessarily delaying to move a piece touched. Either principal who so acts after he has been warned of the consequences and requested to desist, shall forfeit the game.

During a game, neither player (unless accompanied by his opponent) shall be permitted to leave the room without sufficient reason or without receiving his opponent's assent.

Any spectator giving warning, either by sign, sound, or remark, on any of the games, whether played or pending, shall be ordered from the room during the match, and play may be discontinued until such offending person has retired.

14. Match Games

A match between equals, wins and draws to count, should consist of an even number of games, so that each player would have the Black men—that is, the "first move"—the same number of times.

15. Enforcement of the Laws

The principal who violates these laws must submit to the

prescribed penalty, and his opponent is equally bound to exact the same.

16. Unforeseen Disputes

Should any dispute arise that cannot be satisfactorily settled by the preceding laws, a written statement of facts must be sent to a disinterested arbiter, having knowledge of the game, and being acceptable to both parties, whose decision shall be final.

APPENDIX II

Variants of Checkers

In addition to the customary way of playing checkers, there are several interesting variants. These include:

Spanish checkers. Played the same way as ordinary checkers, with the following exceptions.

1. With a choice of captures, a player must capture the maximum possible of adverse pieces.

2. A King may move any distance along an open diagonal and capture by jumping to an adjacent vacant square beyond an adverse piece which is any distance away on that King's diagonal.

3. The double corner is at the players' left.

Italian checkers. A single piece cannot capture a King. When a player has a choice, he must take the King rather than a single piece and must take the maximum number of the adverse pieces and also the most powerful of the adverse pieces. The double corner is at the players' left.

Polish checkers. Played on a 10x10 square board with 20 pieces for each player. The single piece can move forward only but may capture backward or forward. A single piece that reaches the King row by capturing and finds an adverse piece adjacent (with a vacant square beyond) must continue jumping. A single piece becomes a King (called "Queen" in Polish) only when it can stop on the King's row.

A piece must take the maximum possible number of adverse pieces. The King ("Queen") is like a chess Bishop in that it may move diagonally; but the King may land on *any* square on the diagonal beyond the captured piece. The King must land where he is best able to continue jumping, when there is a choice.

German checkers. Same as Polish checkers except that it is played on an ordinary 8x8 square board with 12 pieces each.

Russian checkers. Same as German checkers except that a choice of capture is allowed.

Turkish checkers. All 64 squares are used, and each player has 16 pieces. The single piece moves one square forward, diagonally or sideways, but always captures by leaping the enemy's piece on an adjacent square and landing on the next unoccupied square. A piece must take a maximum number of pieces.

The King moves any distance in any direction and jumps to the adjacent vacant square. Each captured piece is removed from the board before the capturing piece continues jumping. This may make additional captures possible.

Montreal or *Quebec checkers.* Played on a 12x12 square board with all 72 dark squares used and with 30 men each.

INDEX

Self-improvement books available from:

WILSHIRE BOOK COMPANY

8721 Sunset Blvd.
Hollywood, California 90069

Send for our free 116-page illustrated catalog of self-help books.

WILSHIRE SELF-IMPROVEMENT LIBRARY

Notes

Notes

Notes